THE TERRIBLE TRUTH
ABOUT LAWYERS

THE TERRIBLE
TRUTH
ABOUT LAWYERS

What Every Business Person
Needs to Know

Mark H. McCormack

COLLINS
8 Grafton Street, London W1
1987

William Collins Sons & Co. Ltd
London · Glasgow · Sydney · Auckland
Toronto · Johannesburg

BRITISH LIBRARY CATALOGUING IN PUBLICATION DATA

McCormack, Mark
The terrible truth about lawyers: what
every business person needs to know.
1. Commercial law – Great Britain
I. Title
344.106'7'02465   KD1629

ISBN 0-00-217869-9

First published in Great Britain 1987

Photoset in Linotron Sabon by
Rowland Phototypesetting Ltd
Bury St Edmunds, Suffolk
Made and printed in Great Britain
by Robert Hartnoll (1985) Ltd., Bodmin, Cornwall

To my father, Ned Hume McCormack, who urged me to go to law school, correctly assessing that, if nothing else, it would help me to think more logically and to be more aware of the importance of the written and spoken word.

To the three most important legacies that I have in the world:

> My son Breck, a lawyer with IMG, who is struggling valiantly and effectively to move within 'the wall of molasses';

> My son Todd, an educator and executive, who is becoming ever more aware of the necessity to teach the values and workings of the 'real' world;

> My daughter Leslie, a student at William and Mary, who is learning so graciously and well that there is much more to our lives than can be taught or learned in the academic milieu, and

To my wife Betsy, who helps keep my feet squarely on the ground, keeps reminding me to stop and 'smell the roses', and, quite simply, makes it all worthwhile.

CONTENTS

ACKNOWLEDGEMENTS

It would be impossible to write a book like this without acknowledgements and thanks to a lot of very special people:

To the professors at Yale Law School, who gave me my first exposure to the 'Law';

To the partners at Arter, Hadden, Wykoff & Van Duzer – especially Clyde Comstock, Clint Horn, Jim Stewart and Tom Koykka – who taught me how the 'Law' worked in the real world and gave me the chance to try the sports management business.

To Bob Burton, Jay Lafave and Bill Carpenter, who taught me and are still teaching me what conscience and the 'Law' really mean;

To Laurie Roggenburk, Leah Detwiller, Sarah Wooldridge and Judy Stott, who tirelessly helped me and/or put up with me during the preparation of this book;

To Larry Shames, a brilliant and responsive collaborator, without whom this book could never have been completed; and

To Arnold Palmer, who in the last analysis made everything possible.

Discourage litigation. Persuade your neighbours to compromise whenever you can. Point out to them how the nominal winner is often a real loser – in fees, expenses, and waste of time. As a peace-maker, the lawyer has a superior opportunity of being a good man. There will be business enough.

ABRAHAM LINCOLN

The first thing we do, let's kill all the lawyers.

WILLIAM SHAKESPEARE

PREFACE

George Bernard Shaw once quipped, 'All professions are conspiracies against the laity.'

Now, I don't know how seriously Shaw meant his remark to be taken. I do know, however, that it comes pretty close to summarizing the feeling that many people – maybe most people – have about the men and women who make up the profession of law.

In the general view, lawyers are a clubby group who, with the benefit of an arcane body of knowledge and under the smokescreen of an elaborate system of professional courtesies and rituals, look out for their own – at the expense of the rest of us.

Successful lawyers wield more power than most people. They make more money than most people. Typically, they are called in after ordinary reason has failed, when people are already angry, disillusioned, and ready for a fight. For all these and other reasons, lawyers are the targets of an enormous amount of resentment.

Much of that resentment is well deserved. The terrible truth is that lawyers – to be blunt – tend to be a real pain in the neck.

In a world where time is money, lawyers are masters at stalling.

In business contexts, where clear communication is crucial, lawyers hide behind mumbo jumbo that nobody else understands.

In a society where justice, in theory at least, is held up as the highest ideal, lawyers are always looking for technical and sometimes dubious means of bending the law to their advantage.

We all know it shouldn't be that way.

All but the most cynical among us believe it doesn't *have* to be that way.

But, in the meantime, that's the way it is.

I know. I'm a lawyer myself – albeit a non-practising one. But back before I took a lucky $500 and launched the company that became International Management Group, I *did* practise law, and the experience has proved invaluable both to my understanding of human nature and to my career in business.

IMG is now a worldwide company with annual revenues approaching half a billion dollars. A global industry of sports management and sports marketing has sprouted up around us. I'm proud to say we are still the leaders in our original business: representing celebrity athletes like Arnold Palmer, Muhammad Ali, Bjorn Borg, Billie Jean King, Martina Navratilova, Herschel Walker, Jean-Claude Killy, and many others.

But IMG has expanded far beyond its original mission. We produce and/or sell television programming for Wimbledon, the National Football League, the US Tennis and US Golf associations, and the National Collegiate Athletics Association. More than fifty major corporations use our marketing consulting services all over the world. We have been advisers to the organizing committees of both the Winter and Summer Olympics of 1988, and we have represented entities as far removed from sport as the Nobel Foundation, the Vatican, and the Van Cliburn International Piano Competition.

In all our far-flung enterprises, we deal in situations where the stakes are high, the personalities often volatile, and litigation an all-too-frequent ending to a story that started off happily. In my role as chairman and CEO, I have found that being a trained lawyer as well as a practising businessman has given me a dual perspective that has proved enormously useful.

I have sat on both sides of the lawyer–client relationship, so I know how both sides feel when legal fees start to escalate.

I am acquainted with the use of legalese as a dodge and as a weapon, as an intimidator and as a stalling device.

I understand the deep temperamental differences that often make lawyers and businessmen drive each other crazy, and I have learned ways to deal with those differences so that businessmen and lawyers can work more smoothly as a team.

As a lawyer, I am aware of the things that lawyers don't want their clients to know. As a client, I am familiar with the questions and complaints that laymen have for and about lawyers, but are either too intimidated to ask or don't know how to bring up.

Most basically of all, I have come to realize that a legal education does not a lawyer make, and that, on the other hand, one doesn't *need* a legal education to think the way a lawyer thinks – or to protect oneself effectively against lawyers.

The education I received at Yale Law School was a fine one, and I am grateful for it. Yale takes the training of attorneys about as far as it can be taken in three classroom years – and if that sounds like a backhanded compliment, it is.

The fact is, a law school graduate, on the day he or she picks up the sheepskin, is like a learner driver who has studied everything about the science of driving but has never driven a car. In both cases, the heart of the matter lies not in abstract knowledge but in the sharpening of innate talents by experience.

And you can't pick up that kind of intuition at school – not at Yale, not anywhere.

The reason is that the study of law entails so many hundreds of hours of rote memorization and blind absorption that there simply isn't much time left over for the study of what makes people tick. The technical side of law is so complicated and abstruse that it takes up about 95 per cent of most law students' time; that leaves about 5 per cent for learning about *people* – and it's people, after all, who make the laws, interpret the laws, and have no choice but to be bound by the laws.

The irony is that not only is the technical aspect of law of little interest to non-lawyers, it's not even that compelling to the majority of lawyers themselves, once they have got

11

through law school and been called to the bar. Practising attorneys don't *remember* all that stuff; they look things up in a book when they have to – or, better yet, they have a clerk do their research *for* them. And of course it's the client who pays a fat hourly fee while the attorney has his memory refreshed.

In the real world, then, it's not the technical details that are most germane to the practice of law; it's the *human* side – the shrewd yet sympathetic understanding of human conflicts and human motivations, the honing of the powers of persuasion, the mastery of the nuances of logic and argument – that is the meat of what a lawyer needs to know. And in *those* areas, a savvy client can meet an attorney on even terms. It is the human skills that get practical results. Those are the universal tools that a successful lawyer should have in common with a successful businessman, a successful scientist, a successful *anyone*.

They are skills that no law school can teach, and they are precisely what this book is about.

In this volume, I'll be speaking both as an attorney and as a client. If my sympathies generally fall on the client's side, it's because as a businessman I have found that all too often it's the lawyers who:

1. gum up the works;
2. get people mad at each other;
3. make business procedures much more expensive than they need to be; and
4. now and then hash up what had seemed a perfectly workable arrangement.

Accordingly, I would say that probably the best way to deal with lawyers is not to deal with them.

I think, quite frankly, that the best agreements I have ever made have been those with no contract or written agreement attached to them – no legalese, no what-ifs, no fine print.

The first and most crucial of these agreements was a hand-

12

shake deal I made with Arnold Palmer back in early 1960 – a handshake that, more than any other single event, ushered in the era of mutual profit between professional athletes and professional managers. Basically, Arnold and I had an understanding. We were reasonable people. We trusted each other and had a common goal. Our arrangement was simplicity itself.

In the twenty-seven years since that handshake, a lot has happened that neither Arnold nor I could have anticipated. But for all that has changed, we have rarely had to take more than a minute or two to resolve any issue.

For example, when I first started representing Arnold, our arrangement called for a commission based on his gross income – and that included *all* his income, right on up to the interest on his savings account. At the beginning of our relationship, Arnold's savings account was the only investment he had, and the interest on it came to about $120 a year. Sometime later, Arnold's interest income alone was running into six figures annually, and we were still taking our commission.

One day Arnold said, 'You know, Mark, we never really had in mind that you'd be getting this kind of money from investment income, especially since you already commissioned most of the money before it went into the accounts.' Now, sticking to the literal facts of our agreement, I could have argued. But the simple fact was, he was *right*. So I agreed, we shook hands on our revised understanding, and that was that.

If business deals could always be so amicably concluded, there would be little need for lawyers, right?

Wrong, unfortunately.

Because, even assuming the best faith and most congenial of circumstances, there is still the grim but real possibility that one party or the other will be hit by the proverbial bus.

People change. People forget. People die, but deals, especially when the stakes get high, live on and on. So the terrible truth is that the lawyers cannot be kept out of the picture forever. Even deals that start with a handclasp and a

13

big smile eventually take on the baggage of signed documents and memos back and forth.

But here's the crucial point, which I think of as one of my axioms:

McCormack's Axiom of Good Contracts

If a lawyer is serving his client faithfully and well, and if a client is using his lawyer effectively and appropriately, then a legal contact should allow for the same flexibility and ongoing goodwill as a handshake deal.

Lew Wasserman, the chairman of MCA, once told me that he thought of a legal contract as no more than a piece of paper setting forth the foundation from which settlement discussions might commence. In other words, the contract — no matter how much the lawyers hum and haw over details, and how shamelessly they murder the English language in the name of legal precision — can only be an *approximate* description of the understanding between the parties.

A *deal is a living thing*, a contract is static. And the purpose of a contract is to *support* the living, evolving deal, not supplant it.

To put it another way: although law schools don't preach this, **lawyers are in a service business**, and what they service is other people's hard-won understandings. Since professional arrogance is an occupational hazard among lawyers, they don't like to think of it that way. But it's really that simple: lawyers, in typical business situations, are called in *after the fact*, to consolidate and safeguard the work done by someone else, namely the person who made the deal. If both the lawyer and the client would keep that in mind, things could run relatively smoothly.

The situation is more complicated, of course, when the attorneys are brought in not merely to formalize a good-faith deal, but to fight out a dispute. In those instances, the so-called adversary relationship can become a fully-fledged war.

A client's sense of justice can all too easily become warped by a hunger for revenge.

An attorney's professional judgement can all too often be clouded by an ego-driven obsession with winning.

Time, money, peace of mind, and even self-respect are squandered in the name of ... what? Getting even? Proving a point? Trying to get rich quick on the quirky largesse of a jury?

Lawsuits, by their very nature, are unpleasant proceedings, and nothing I could say would change that. But I happen to believe that the inherent unpleasantness and expense of litigation are made far worse by certain flaws in Western legal systems and by certain unconscionable elements in the standard operating procedures of attorneys.

What are those flaws and those inequities? Just to name a few:

— the 'time charge' method of billing, whereby lawyers charge clients up to $500 or even more per hour, *irrespective of whether their work produces any result whatsoever, or even if it was really necessary*;

— the 'contingency fee' system, which creates a no-lose scenario for plaintiffs and thereby encourages frivolous suits with shoot-the-moon requests for damages;

— the 'deep pockets' psychology of juries, which leads to verdicts based not on culpability or reasonable redress for harms, but on jurors' perceptions of how much the defendant — typically a corporation — can afford.

Those things make me mad — and part of my reason for writing this book is that I want them to make *you* mad, too.

I don't intend to get up on a soapbox and hold forth about how things ought to be. But I can read you chapter and verse — through real-life stories that involve IMG and the people we deal with — on the ways in which bad laws and bad lawyering cost us money, as business people and as taxpayers.

I can show how the 'fine-print mentality' hamstrings us as executives.

I can demonstrate how the fear of liability cripples innovation.

I can illustrate the ways in which competing in the courtroom hampers and perverts the principle of competing in the marketplace.

If this book contributes at all to the kind of indignation that brings about constructive change, then I feel I have done something worthwhile.

Our main subject, though, is not law and lawyers as they should be, but as they are — imperfect, infuriating, human. And the issues we will deal with are mainly practical ones.

For the layman: **How to get the best punch from the legal pound.** How to judge when you can avoid lawyers altogether. How to get around the *other* person's attorney. How to make sure your own lawyer remains responsive and accountable. How to integrate lawyers into an effective business team.

For attorneys, I hope to provide some useful feedback from the world beyond their panelled offices: What simple, common-sense steps can lawyers take **to maintain their client's loyalty?** When should an attorney yield to a client's business savvy and set aside his own, more technical, and often more belligerent expertise? When does an eager-beaver businessman desperately *need* an attorney to save him from himself?

Beyond these specific issues for clients and practitioners, there is another, more subtle kind of advice that I hope the reader will carry away from these pages. People are funny. They gripe about lawyers, they make snide jokes about lawyers, yet secretly they wish they could be more *like* lawyers.

They wish they could be more effective in arguments, more cool-headed and dispassionate in the midst of confrontations. They wish they could remain suavely logical even when angry, and they wish they had the knack of using that logic like a fist, a sledgehammer, or a scalpel.

People wish, in short, that they could win more arguments,

prevail in more conflicts, and enjoy the confidence of knowing they can stand up for their point of view.

I like to think this book will help people – and even attorneys – accomplish those things a little more effectively.

PART I

---

*The War Between Lawyers
and Clients*

1

What We're Up Against

Life Inside the 'Wall of Molasses'

I didn't write this book to win friends, and over the course of the next couple of hundred pages, I'll have some very uncomplimentary things to say about attorneys.

I have laid in more than a quarter century's worth of war stories showing lawyers at their most stubborn, adversarial and obstructive.

I have formulated some advice that will put clients on a more equal footing with their attorneys, and that will probably cost attorneys money.

But I would like to make it clear that, while I may be critical of certain features of our legal system and of the general run of legal practitioners, I'm not fundamentally unsympathetic towards attorneys. If most of us, as laymen, are up against ridiculously high legal costs and ridiculously slow legal actions, lawyers have troubles of their own.

Lawyers, like dentists, are well aware that no one wants to have any more to do with them than he or she absolutely has to. They go through life knowing that they are complained about and mistrusted by most of the general populace. Toughest of all, they spend their arduous careers labouring inside a 'wall of molasses'.

Just what is this wall of molasses?

It is probably the most apt metaphor I have ever heard for describing the Western system of jurisprudence. Like justice Western-style, molasses is gummy, slow, and more or less opaque.

21

Once you make contact with the wall of molasses, you can't move up, you can't move down, and you can't move from side to side.

Most horrifying of all, you usually find you can't even get back out again.

Anyone who has ever been involved in even the most routine legal procedure can testify how exhausting it is to make any progress through that wall. Well, that's what lawyers are up against every day of their working lives – and I would argue that even those who pull princely livings out of the wall of molasses are not immune to its frustrations.

The poignant part is that no attorney-to-be starts off thinking of the law that way. Future lawyers are taught in terms of elegant abstractions and nifty-sounding Latin phrases. Law schools excel in highfalutin rhetoric.

Only after graduation do young attorneys come to the depressing realization that **90 per cent of what they were taught in academia will never be used in practice; and, conversely, 90 per cent of what they need to know in practice was never taught to them at school.**

Notes from Underground

Let me tell you about the incident which, more than any other, brought that hard truth home to me.

I was an eager young associate at the large and highly reputed Cleveland firm known then as Arter, Hadden, Wykoff, and Van Duzer – the oldest law firm, by the way, west of the Appalachian Mountains. Like any serious-minded fledgling fresh out of Yale, I was perfectly willing to put in sixteen-hour days, reading until my eyes went bleary, doing research, and writing memos until, quite literally, language simply stopped making sense because of my utter exhaustion.

But I liked to think that there was some logical connection between the amount of time a given procedure took, and the intrinsic value of that procedure.

Then the *Geffine v. Doyle* case came along.

A man named Victor Geffine had brought a suit against a

Canadian promoter named John Doyle and a number of co-defendants, one of whom – the Steel Company of Canada – was a client of ours. The entire basis of what went on to become a multimillion-dollar action was this. Geffine alleged that at some point Doyle had said to him, in essence: 'If you will go along with me and together we are able to interest steel companies in the development of iron ore properties on which I hold the leases, I will make you a rich man.'

Geffine claimed that this statement constituted a contract and that Doyle had reneged. Doyle claimed that he had never made the statement or even implied such a promise.

In preparing to defend the suit, it was my task to go through all the files pertaining to any business that Doyle and Geffine had ever done together, *or* that Doyle had done with the Steel Company of Canada in which Geffine might possibly have been mentioned, *or* that Geffine had done with any of the co-defendants in which *Doyle* had possibly been mentioned.

Now, how long would you expect such a process to take? A week? A month?

Well, it took a year and a half – of my young life.

As it happened, some of the files, years old, were stored in the sub-subbasement of a garage in the Dominion Square Building in Montreal. Others were stashed away in a cellar in St John's, Newfoundland. For eighteen months I lived like a mole, like Dostoevsky's 'underground man'.

Our client spent tens of thousands of dollars keeping me in plane tickets and hotel rooms so that I could sit in Canadian cellars, read in terrible light with my coat on, and eat expense-account dinners alone.

To make matters worse, I was painfully aware that the whole grand noble sweep of my law school education was now focused on one tiny question of the sort that is routinely argued among six-year-olds: *Did someone promise something to so-and-so, or did he not?*

The capper was that the whole object of this eighteen-month scavenger hunt was *not* to find anything!

It wasn't my job, you understand, to prove that Doyle *hadn't* promised anything to Geffine, but only to confirm that no documents existed proving that he *had*. Sure enough, at the end of my research, when I confidently reported to the partners that no compromising papers could be found, it was decided to call the plaintiff's bluff. We told Geffine's attorneys that settlement was out of the question and we would see them in court. The suit gently vanished.

And I was left to ask myself the incredibly simple but too often overlooked question that *every* lawyer and *every* client should ask himself with regard to *every* legal process:

Was it worth it?

That depends, of course, on how you reckon. Measured against the millions of dollars that would have been at risk had the case been tried, yes, my time and the client's money were well spent.

But considering that the action was without merit to begin with, and that 99 per cent of what I had learned in law school was going unused as I slogged through hundreds of hours of mechanical chores, well, I'm not so sure.

In another sense, however, the experience of that solitary confinement in northeastern basements was enormously valuable because it helped convince me that the pure practice of law was not for me, that I craved the more freewheeling eventfulness of business.

I believed then – and I believe now – that a good legal education provides an incomparable background in mental discipline and logical thinking.

But *Geffine v. Doyle* taught me that, in the real world, lawyerly discipline and logic are usually applied to issues of stupefying pettiness! That realization, in turn, led me to formulate another axiom:

McCormack's Axiom of Demystification

Once you get past the mumbo jumbo, the overwhelming majority of what lawyers do is basically high-level research and make-work paper-shuffling that takes too damn long and costs too damn much for what you get.

So I sympathize with my brothers and sisters of the working bar, whose professional lives will consist of *Geffine v. Doyle* many times over. I say to them, sincerely, Good luck — but don't try to kid me about the deep mysteries of your expertise!

The Other Side of the Fence

These days, of course, I play a very different role when complex and protracted lawsuits like *Geffine v. Doyle* come along. Now I'm either the one who's suing or the one who's being sued. Either way, I'm the one who's footing the bill as the legal fees mount up.

I have thought long and hard about ways to minimize legal bills, not to mention disruption of business. And I have evolved a policy of asking myself a series of questions — all variations on one crucial query: is it worth it? — *before* spending dollar one on lawyers or initiating any sort of legal action.

Going through the following questions calmly and open-mindedly is the best way I have been able to decide when I do or do not need a lawyer, or when a dispute should or should not be legally pursued:

1. Does this problem *necessarily* call for a *legal* resolution, or can it be handled in some other way — e.g., by a business manoeuvre or negotiation?
2. If IMG is thinking of suing, is there a reasonable chance of an award? Is the other side broke? Can the other side *present itself* as broke? Is the principle at stake so crucial that I can't afford *not* to sue?
3. If IMG is being sued, is there an affordable and honourable way to settle or, better still, to persuade the other side to drop the action?
4. When one has the choice of initiating a legal action, is the net result — figuring in time, money, anger, anxiety and ruined relationships — likely to be more advantageous than *doing nothing at all*?

Let's look briefly at the implications of each of these questions.

1. LEGAL GAMBIT, BUSINESS PARRY

Back in 1984, Trans World International, the IMG entity that produces television sports programming, was sued by the US Ski Team for allegedly using some film footage without permission.

This was a bizarre suit, for several reasons. First of all, the footage was used as part of our *Sarajevo '84* coverage, in a preview series for the 1984 Sarajevo Winter Olympics, and it constituted some of the most advantageous exposure the ski team had ever enjoyed. It was a boon to the ski team's fund-raising efforts.

Second, TWI *had* gotten releases from the individual skiers involved.

Third, TWI and the USST had, up to that point, shared a friendly and mutually profitable relationship, and until the day the complaint landed on our general counsel's desk, there was no hint of any sort of trouble in the air.

So what was going on?

What was going on was that the ski team was having internal political problems, and had broken into warring factions, one of which was hostile to TWI.

But here's the point: **if our company had responded to the complaint only in strict legal terms, we would never have known that, and so would have been unable to defend ourselves effectively.**

Legal language is so highly stylized that *it conceals as much as it reveals*. To get to the crux of the ski team's grievance against us, I had to resist the panicky, knee-jerk temptation to call in *our* lawyers to deal with *their* lawyers.

Instead, I elected to talk to decision makers within the ski team organization *as a businessman*.

Slowly but surely, without the tension of courtroom drama and the implied threats of legal documents, I was able to learn of the internal power struggle that was the real reason for the conflict. I was advised just to sit tight and wait for the good guys to win – at which point the suit would disappear.

And it did.

So consider the advantages, in this case, of seeking a *business* solution to a problem that seemed at first glance legal.

(a) We saved many thousands of dollars in lawyers' fees.
(b) We spared ourselves the negative publicity of being portrayed — inaccurately — as exploiters of our beloved Olympic athletes.
(c) Perhaps most important, we avoided the ill will of a full-blown legal fight and cemented our relationship with the more reasonable elements within the ski team hierarchy.

For all those reasons, and others that may apply in various cases, one should *always* consider informal, one-to-one solutions *before* tackling a problem on a formal, legal footing.

2. AVOIDING PYRRHIC VICTORIES

If it takes considerable restraint not to call in the lawyers immediately when you are attacked legally, it sometimes takes even greater forbearance not to sue when you know you have been abused.

In those instances, moral indignation combines with an eye for the main chance. You have a tendency to assume that the whole world will sympathize with the wrongs you have suffered, and that society will compensate you in a big way.

To prevent feelings like those from getting the best of my better judgement, I make it a point to take a deep breath and a walk around the block before deciding to sue someone. And I also make it a point to ask myself **not only if law and justice are on my side, but also if I'll be able to collect the money I will presumably be awarded.**

Now, there *are* times when one should sue, irrespective of the likelihood of an award. There are times when a bulldog stance must be struck on behalf of a client, or when a strong signal must be sent to a business partner who isn't playing fair.

But, frankly, those times are relatively rare. Making points for the sake of making points is the role of essayists and philosophers; the business of business is to get things done.

And I must say there are few things in my business life that frustrate me more than going to all the trouble and expense of bringing a suit and winning a suit, and then walking away empty-handed.

To gain an idea of just how futile and irritating this can be, consider a case we pursued a few years back on behalf of golfer Donna Caponi.

Donna had an endorsement contract with a club manufacturer called Swinging Promotions. Suffice it to say that Swinging Promotions was not the most successful sporting goods company in history, and it eventually found itself with a warehouse full of Donna Caponi autographed golf clubs and a commitment it didn't feel like honouring. We tried reasoning; we tried threatening; we sued.

As so often happens, Swinging Productions' first tactic was to stall. The company's lawyers concocted all sorts of pre-trial motions, argued over jurisdiction, and pulled all the standard delaying stunts.

After costing us some six months and $20,000 or so, the company suddenly did an about face: it agreed to move the case out of full-scale litigation and submit it to an arbitrator.

This was the first reasonable thing Swinging Promotions had done, and we should have realized there was more to the move than met the eye. But we went ahead with the arbitration. We flew witnesses from California to Buffalo, New York, where the proceeding was being held. We juggled Donna Caponi's tournament schedule so she could testify on her own behalf.

And sure enough, we were awarded everything we asked for in the arbitration.

Whereupon we were informed that Swinging Promotions had filed for bankruptcy in the meantime.

There was no money to collect. And we weren't particularly interested in taking our award in the form of golf clubs.

So why had we bothered? We knew all along that Swinging Promotions was a shaky company at best. There was no great principle at stake, and we were not likely to do repeat business with this outfit anyway. About the only positive result of our action was that we had demonstrated to a client that we would go to the wall on her behalf.

As a business gesture, an important point was made. But was it worth all the trouble and expense, and was pursuing a pyrrhic lawsuit the best way to assure our client we were with her?

Frankly, I don't think so. Chalk that one up as a learning experience. If I had it to do over again, I wouldn't do it.

3. PAY THE TWO DOLLARS

Nobody likes to be shaken down. Nothing is more in keeping with human nature than to adopt a defensive posture when someone is assailing you. In the great majority of civil lawsuits, therefore, people will vigorously defend themselves even when they know they're flat, dead wrong.

But let's not be naive. **Justice is only one factor in a lawsuit, and often not the most compelling.** Being right doesn't necessarily mean you'll win, and there are times when its easier, cheaper and more dignified to settle. Sometimes, as much as it hurts, the rational decision is to swallow your losses and get on with your life.

A number of years ago, IMG hired an 'expert' to be a consultant on a sports event we were staging for TV. This 'expert' did less than nothing for us. He promised us contacts who, it turned out, barely knew who he was. He had no ideas. He slowed us down by inserting himself in the middle of certain decisions and then being unresponsive.

We cancelled his contract for nonperformance, and he sued us.

Here was a case where we were morally in the right but legally exposed. It is incredibly difficult to prove that someone didn't perform a service, when that service is as loosely defined as 'consulting'. We knew that if we went to trial, this individual could produce a log of phone calls answered, meetings attended, and so forth; that he *accomplished* nothing would be nearly impossible to demonstrate. Additionally, the psychology of juries would almost certainly favour the poor defenceless individual against the big monolithic corporation.

We bought this person off for several thousand dollars. That's not a phrase in official use in law school, but there's no prettier way to put it. They don't teach you in law school that *often the choice comes down to paying the plaintiff or paying the lawyers*. We made what I believe was a sound business decision.

By settling, we put a cap on our losses. By *not* settling, we would have remained vulnerable both to the running up of huge legal fees and to the possibility of an off-the-wall judgment.

For those reasons I urge everyone to put aside ego and moral indignation, and to be open to the possibility of settling and settling early.

4. THE PASSIVE OPTION

Everyone knows that a defendant in a criminal trial can plead either innocent or guilty.

Not everyone knows that there is a third option: nolo contendere, or 'no contest'. A plea of nolo contendere in the US means basically that one neither admits blame nor claims innocence, but simply lets the matter rest with the wisdom and mercy of the court.

In other words, one chooses to do nothing.

Now, given that our whole system of law is based on *argument*, the concept of *nolo contendere* is intriguing and a little bit subversive: the whole adversarial process is short-circuited if one side refuses to fight!

Nolo contendere is a concept from criminal law, not civil law. Still, I would argue that in *figurative* terms, the concept of 'no contest' has valuable applications.

There's an old Zen maxim that goes 'Never to argue is never to be wrong'. In business situations, that bromide can be stated even more strongly: not arguing can often make you something of a hero.

For that reason, I would urge anyone who's deciding whether to pursue a lawsuit to consider what I call 'The Passive Option'.

Let's say that our client Chris Evert is hired – some months in advance, of course – to play an exhibition at the grand opening of a new tennis resort. By no bad faith on management's part, the opening is delayed because of construction difficulties, labour problems, or whatever. The company makes a bona fide effort to reschedule Chris for another time, but there are simply no free dates on her calendar. So the tennis resort reneges on its contract.

The resort's management realizes, of course, that they are opening themselves to a lawsuit. Chances are that they are braced for us to sue, whereupon they will try to settle for *part* of what they had intended to pay Chris to play the exhibition.

But what if we don't sue?

What if, after getting Chris's approval, I call the CEO and say, 'I'm sorry your project got off schedule, and we're going to let you walk away from the contract you have with us'?

First of all, the CEO would probably be shocked. *And it is always an advantage in business to be able to surprise someone.*

Second, he would be grateful that we were making his life easier rather than harder, and he would probably feel that he 'owed us one'. Assuming that his company will be around for awhile, we would almost certainly come out ahead in the long run.

Third, since people like to talk about unusual happenings, chances are this CEO would tell other members of his circle about how we let him off the hook, and since *every business is a word-of-mouth business*, this would enhance our reputation for being a good bunch of people to deal with.

Aren't all those advantages better than the expense, uncertainty, and ill will of one more acrimonious and drawn-out lawsuit?

Where Not *to Go for Legal Advice*

Whenever possible, you should think about the above considerations *before* plunging into the 'wall of molasses'.

Further, whenever possible you should at least begin to think about them **before even talking to a lawyer.**

Why?

Because lawyers are educated and programmed to resolve differences by way of the judicial process. This is not simply the way they make their living, it's the lens through which they look at the world.

So you can't expect an attorney to look at a legal problem and see an intuitive, business-based solution.

You can't expect an attorney to look at a case he could probably win and see a battle not worth fighting.

You can't expect an attorney to be overly enthusiastic about The Passive Option when the benefits of doing nothing will accrue only to you and not put a nickel in his pocket.

The terrible truth is that you can't expect an attorney *not* to be an attorney.

And everything that follows in this book will be clearer and more useful if we take a few minutes to explore what being an attorney really means.

2

How Lawyers Got That Way

Is It True All Lawyers Look Alike?

Think about the business people you know.

They probably ran the gamut of personality types. Some are quiet, some are boisterous, some are worriers, some are bold. In their business styles they probably cover the range from conservative-executive to visionary-entrepreneur.

Now think about the lawyers you are acquainted with. Unless I miss my guess, they probably all resemble each other quite a bit.

Chances are they have in common a certain solemnity of aspect and formality of expression, a 'lawyerliness' that shows even in their smallest gestures.

An attorney friend of mine once told me that wherever he goes — even to the hardware store, dressed in jeans and a sweatshirt on a Saturday morning — people say to him, apropos of nothing: 'You're a lawyer, aren't you?'

What accounts for this strong family resemblance shared by the great majority of practising attorneys?

The answer can only be that *there are powerful forces shaping these people on their way to becoming lawyers.*

These forces operate first in law schools, and second, at the associate level in which young attorneys do what amounts to a medieval-style apprenticeship.

What They Do Teach You at Yale Law School

By an interesting coincidence, one of the most stinging indictments ever written about American legal education was written by a professor from Yale Law School.

His name is Charles A. Reich, and in 1970 he published a very popular and influential book called *The Greening of America*. In assessing what he felt was right and wrong about our culture, he started off with the part of that culture he knew most intimately, and this is what he had to say:

> Finding themselves in law school . . . [students] discover that they are expected to become 'argumentative' personalities who listen to what someone else is saying only for the purpose of disagreeing; 'analytic' rather than receptive people, who dominate information rather than respond to it; and intensely competitive and self-assertive as well. Since many of them are not this sort of personality before they start law school, they react initially with anger and despair, and later with resignation . . . In a very real sense, they 'become stupider' during law school, as the range of their imagination is limited, their ability to respond with sensitivity and to receive impressions is reduced, and the scope of their reading and thinking is progressively narrowed.

Say It Ain't So, Joe

It would be nice if I could refute Reich's observations. But I can't. Let's look at a few of his assertions individually.

Are law students expected and in fact pressured to become 'argumentative' personalities? You bet they are.

The whole thrust of their classroom training is geared towards the inculcation of what is known as 'the adversarial turn of mind'.

A case is introduced in class. By their nature, law cases have two sides. It's always Us against Them, Me against You. Whatever the other side says, you *have* to disagree.

34

Not only that, but if the professor tells you, halfway through a case, to shift your allegiance to the other side of the question, you have to argue *that* side just as deftly and with as much *semblance* of commitment as you argued the other.

In real life, this would be called hypocrisy; among law students, it's known as survival. And it gets to be an intellectual habit.

But law students aren't trained to do battle only against other law students; they're constantly put on the spot to argue against professors as well.

This creates just one problem: since law cases can be argued in any number of ways, no matter *what* the student says, the teacher can show him to be wrong – in front of a hundred or so of his peers.

This way of teaching is known as the Socratic method. It can also be thought of as **The Professor Always Wins, and the Student Lives in Terror.**

Make no mistake, *terror is an integral part of the law school experience, and the long-term consequence of that terror is to make it very difficult for lawyers to admit when they've made an error or when they simply don't know something. The ultimate sin is being at a loss for words.*

Law school has taught them to hide uncertainty at any cost. It has also taught them what a powerful weapon intimidation can be.

Finally, law school *does* tend to make people narrower in their interests, just because it's so damn difficult and so relentlessly competitive.

People who go to law school are accustomed to being academic stars. Chances are they were at the top of the heap all through school and university. Suddenly, for the first time ever, they find themselves in the middle of the pack. There's always someone smarter, someone willing to study an hour longer.

Maybe Professor Reich is a shade harsh in saying that people 'become stupider' in law school. But there's no denying that they leave parts of themselves behind.

35

You can't read novels or practise the 'cello when you're fighting for your life.

And in dealing with lawyers, here's something important to keep in mind:

> ### McCormack's Axiom of Delayed Rewards
>
> People who have sacrificed large amounts of time and money to get a professional credential – doctors, lawyers, MBAs – come away ferociously determined to get their investment back with interest – from the system and from you!

Oops, We Forgot to Teach You Lawyering!

The irony is that this three-year stint in purgatory doesn't have a lot to do with turning someone into an attorney. It has to do only with getting one a *degree* so that *in later life one may perhaps develop into a competent practitioner.*

Back around 1960, as you may recall, there was a major brouhaha in the American press when the then President John F. Kennedy nominated his brother Bobby to be attorney general. The president's detractors claimed that the appointment was sheer nepotism, and that the younger Kennedy's background in no way justified such a lofty post.

No one questioned that Bobby Kennedy was brilliant or that his University of Virginia legal education was topnotch. The only problem was that he had never in his life tried a case!

Was the position of chief lawyer for the United States government to be held by someone who had never argued to a jury, never jockeyed for advantage with a judge?

In actual fact, however, *the job of attorney general was the one lawyering position in the country that RFK's education was* perfectly *suited to*!

As attorney general, he wouldn't have to do most of the work that practising lawyers actually spend their time on.

He wouldn't have to go through the sticky business of soliciting and dealing with clients.

He wouldn't have to keep a billing chart or worry about a payroll.

He wouldn't have to fret over courtroom tactics because he'd have a staff that would actually try the cases.

What Bobby Kennedy *would* have to do is exactly *the one and only thing* he had been taught to do at school: think legally.

It would be his job to analyze the cogent points of law and justice in a given appellate or legislative process, and to make judgments about the meaning and implications of legal theory and precedent. *That* RFK could do as well as anybody.

So the moral of the story is this: a good legal education prepares you to pass the bar and to be attorney general. For anything in between, you're basically on your own, so lots of luck!

What's Left Out

The rest of this book is essentially devoted to the things you *don't* learn in law school – the intuitive skills of reading people and devising solutions in order to enhance business or personal opportunities – so I won't labour the point. However, consider briefly just a couple of the elements that the standard law school education either glosses over or omits entirely.

1. THE BASIC LAWYERING SKILLS

As usually defined, the four basic skills that every practising attorney needs to have are: interviewing, counselling, negotiating and drafting.

Interviewing has to do with early client contact, getting to know the client's needs and goals, being clear on what you can or cannot accomplish on the client's behalf; and of course with winning the business in the first place.

Counselling is the giving of appropriate advice in an appropriate manner, based on a good working knowledge of the applicable laws and *also* on a sound reading of the client's particular situation.

Negotiating entails a host of strategies, including decisions about when to be cooperative and when intransigent, when to settle and when to fight to the bitter end.

Drafting refers to writing contracts and other legal documents.

As I have said, these are the bedrock lawyering skills. Amazingly enough, *they are not generally taught in law school.* If this strikes you as bizarre, it is. But any candid law school graduate will tell you it's the terrible truth.

How is it possible that the absolutely basic skills of a profession can be neglected in the course of three years' professional education?

Essentially, it's because most law school professors are brilliant men and women whose interest is in the twists, turns and nuances of what is known as Black Letter Law – law as it is written in the statute books, not as it is bent and sometimes mangled by the exigencies of real life.

Law school professors are admirably equipped to teach reasoning and theory. But it is the rare academic who has the foggiest notion of what really goes on in the trenches. So the fact remains that **law school doesn't teach people the things they'll be doing day in, day out, as lawyers.**

2. THE REALITIES OF LAW FIRM MANAGEMENT AND ECONOMICS

Though lawyers seem to chafe at having it put this way, a law firm is essentially a store, a retail operation.

Like any business, a law firm offers a product, the sale of which, it is hoped, will cover the payroll and the overheads, with some profit left over for the owners – in this case, the partners.

In recent years, the running of law firms has become so complicated that there are people who specialize in it – nonlawyers who come in to manage the store. Law firm economics are complex enough to be the subject of surveys by Big Eight accounting firms and other independent auditing concerns.

For all that, *law schools teach virtually nothing about how law firms really work*. Perhaps they don't want to deal with such squalid subjects as paying the rent and covering the utilities, vying for business and dealing with clients who stiff you.

But there is a thin line between idealism and hypocrisy, and let's face it, Yale Law, Harvard Law, and all the rest are essentially top-level trade schools. So why not teach what really makes the trade go round? As of now, the subject is anathema.

Pilgrim's Progress

One of the more humane developments in the history of education was the introduction of the use of cadavers in medical schools. Future doctors could slice-and-dice to their hearts' content, and no one would get hurt.

They could work by trial-and-error, and keep going till they got it right. By the time the doctors touched a living patient, they knew which was the liver and which was the spleen.

There are no cadavers in law school, and, in the typical instance, a law graduate receives a diploma without ever having had real responsibility for a flesh-and-blood client. Not till leaving college does a young attorney stick a toe in the waters of actual practice.

But 'sticking in a toe' is not really what fledgling attorneys do; it's more that they are suddenly thrown in way over their heads, and left to sink or swim.

The Cases No One Wants

In my own experience at Arter, Hadden, the immersion consisted of being handed nearly a hundred 'subrogation cases', and being told to take care of them – with a minimum of supervision.

Subrogation cases have to do with insurance matters; essentially, they are property-damage defence suits in which the insurance companies pay a settlement but the insured is

39

responsible for the deductible. Since the 'subrogation' part only concerns the deductible, these suits are small potatoes, and law firms take them on basically as an accommodation to their insurance company clients.

What better way to break in new associates than to bury them in actions where the firm's exposure is minimal, and none of the partners wants the business anyway?

These subrogation actions taught me plenty. They dragged me down from the ivory tower of Yale, and cast me into the pit of sheriff's auctions in and around Cleveland, where repossessed furniture was routinely sold off to cover the cost of an award.

Far from the academic milieu, where arguments were won on the basis of elegant logic and diligent preparation, I now found myself in rough-and-tumble settings where battles were fought by needling, bluffing, intimidation – and sometimes just by seeing who could scream the loudest.

I was confronted with the sort of gritty dilemmas that no law school professor had ever lectured about:

What did you do if your client didn't show up for a trial?

How did you respond if the other side out-and-out lied, it was obvious as hell, everybody knew it, and it couldn't be proved?

How did you handle it when a jury returned a decision that was utterly inscrutable except in terms of prejudice?

How did you get to sleep at night when you *lost*?

The Rude Awakening

Being confronted with situations like those is part of the initiation and culture shock that everyone goes through on the way to becoming a fully-fledged professional.

And every layman who wishes to understand what makes lawyers tick should understand the effect that that culture shock has on tender-hearted young attorneys.

Some lawyers never quite recover from the disillusionment that attends the first rude rush of actual practice, and they quickly take on a pragmatic cynicism that will help them flourish in our far-from-perfect system. I'm sure we've all met lawyers like that.

Others resolve to keep their ideals intact and to battle the status quo even while being embroiled in it. This is a rarer breed, but it does exist.

And still others begin quickly to wonder if they really want to be practising attorneys after all.

I fell into that final category, though I have no regrets at all about the time, effort and money that went into making me a lawyer in the first place. My legal background affords me certain pleasures, not the least of which is the privilege of being able to pass along to the nonlawyer some inside information that his or her own attorney might be just as happy not to share. . . .

3

What Lawyers Don't Want Their Clients to Know

One of the great half-true maxims of all time is 'Knowledge is power'.

In fact, knowledge can *become* power, but *only if it is wedded to sufficient strength and practical savvy so that it can be put to use.*

This observation puts me in mind of a story about a client of ours, the great running back Herschel Walker. When Herschel was at college, he had a habit of glancing quickly, as he came out of the huddle, towards the spot he'd be hitting on his next carry.

A coach pointed out to the future Heisman Trophy winner that an opposing linebacker might pick up the glance, and so know where to position himself.

Walker shrugged. 'Then he'd be the first guy to get knocked down,' he said.

The moral of the story can be expressed this way:

McCormack's Axiom of Brains and Brawn

Knowledge alone is not sufficient protection against getting steamrollered.

On the other hand, without pertinent knowledge, one is at a serious disadvantage in every power-based transaction. And in lawyer–client relationships, this is what tips the balance in favour of the lawyer.

The Attorney's Edge

Lawyers know two things that the rest of us do not.

One of them is the law. As any honest attorncy will acknowledge, however, they 'know' far less law than you might imagine. The rest they look up as they go along.

Still, attorneys have put in three long years of study, and what their time and trouble has earned them is a monopoly on a certain high-priced commodity.

Just as a law firm is basically a store, the knowledge of legal principles and procedures is essentially a high-ticket product that only lawyers can dispense. That's what it comes down to; once you get past the rhetoric.

The *other* thing that lawyers know – which can and should be known by laymen, too, but which attorneys, for their own profit and convenience, tend to be hush-hush about – is how lawyers actually *operate*.

– How do they behave towards each other, and why?

– What do they say to each other that they wouldn't say to a client?

– How much of your legal pound is used productively and how much pays for oak panelling and handsome leatherbound books that no one but the cleaning lady ever touches?

– What are the questions you should ask your lawyer – whether you're a business person involved in litigation, or an individual seeking counsel in a divorce, or simply a first-time house buyer – *before* you put your fate in his hands?

These are the sorts of things your lawyer would probably just as soon keep you in the dark about. They are the bread-and-butter issues that attorneys talk about among their own, but on which they maintain a staunch silence in the presence of strangers, as if trying to foster the myth that such venal concerns are beneath their notice.

They're not, believe me.

Honour Among Sharks

Let's start with how lawyers deal with each other – a dynamic nicely illustrated by an old joke.

Two lawyers and a priest are cast adrift in a tiny lifeboat in the aftermath of a shipwreck.

Day and night they float without direction on the limitless sea. Their fresh water runs out. They have no food. The sun beats down on them relentlessly.

Finally, on the third day, they drift within sight of an atoll. But as luck would have it, the currents are adverse and they can't get closer than three hundred yards or so. To complicate matters, there is a convoy of sharks scudding back and forth between the atoll and the boat.

Still, one of the lawyers, half mad with thirst, gasps that he just can't take it anymore and leaps out of the boat. He starts swimming ashore while his two companions look on in horror, waiting for him to be torn to bits by the sharks.

Strangely, however, the sharks part ranks and let him swim right past.

'It's a miracle,' says the priest.

'No,' says the other lawyer, 'just professional courtesy.'

Professional courtesy – not a subject you are likely to see offered in many law school catalogues but an absolutely central concept in the life of attorneys.

Codes and Passwords

What exactly *is* professional courtesy, and how exactly does it work?

If you don't know, you shouldn't feel remiss. The fact is, there is something of a tacit conspiracy among attorneys to *prevent* you from knowing.

Professional courtesy is learned not by precept but by osmosis, and its tenets are conveyed from lawyer to lawyer by way of codes and passwords.

Beyond the hocus-pocus, however, the bottom line on professional courtesy is this. **It is a system whereby lawyers**

44

make life easier for themselves and each other, generally at the expense of their clients.

'At a Mutually Convenient Time' . . . Ha, Ha

Let me give you an innocent little example of professional courtesy in action. It has to do with a phrase that anyone who has ever dealt with a lawyer has heard: 'at a mutually convenient time'.

Convenient to whom?

You guessed it.

Back when I was a young associate in Cleveland, I was put in charge of a case that frankly didn't interest me much and that I was ill prepared to present at the appointed time.

I *could* have been prepared to present it, but on the weekend before the action was to be tried, there was a member-guest golf tournament that I was very keen to play in. So I simply picked up the telephone, called the other side's attorney, and asked for a postponement as a professional courtesy. He accommodated me, no questions asked.

So I played my golf game, and prepared the case afterwards.

Shortly before the *second* trial date, however, the other lawyer called *me* on the phone, asking for another delay. I gave it to him, of course. But by this time I felt we knew each other well enough so that a little colleagial ribbing would not be out of line.

'Golf tournament?' I asked.

'No,' he answered with a chuckle. 'Tennis is my game.'

So, between my golf and his tennis, a quite simple procedure took on a sort of Mediterranean tempo and dragged on far longer than it needed to. This sort of thing happens all the time.

Why is it *allowed* to happen?

It is allowed to happen because the clients are generally too damn polite about demanding to know why a given procedure has been postponed.

This is another area in which lawyers typically have the

45

upper hand over clients. **Lawyers are professionals at the art of confrontation; clients tend to be amateurs.**

Clients don't like to risk unpleasantness by asking their own attorney just why the hell this twenty-minute issue is taking six months to resolve.

But they *should* ask.

Every client should ask at the outset of every legal procedure, how long the matter is likely to take to be resolved.

Typically, a lawyer will fudge on the answer, claiming – correctly – that it's impossible to say with any certainty. Still, asking the question sends the message that the client wants a timely resolution – and will take an active stance to get one.

I remember, some years ago, when we were negotiating a very complicated deal for a European exhibition tour on behalf of Muhammad Ali. The tour dates could not be set until a host of issues were resolved, and Ali was impatient. Ali said to us on more than one occasion: 'I don't need to know the fine print and ins-and-outs. *Just tell me the dates.*'

'Ali,' we had no choice but to answer, 'we're doing the best we can. But it's out of our control.'

'But you don't understand,' he said to us. 'I gotta start training. I gotta get psyched up. I gotta know when to stop eating!'

The conversation reminded me that, while the lawyer or the agent is usually more or less content to bide his time, it's the client who is most intimately affected by delays!

If there *are* delays, therefore, a client should *always* insist on knowing the reasons. Don't settle for mealy-mouthed excuses like 'scheduling conflicts'; demand to know what those conflicts *are*.

And if the reasons given don't strike you as persuasive, say so.

Frankly, if a lawyer postponed *my* case because of a golf tournament, I would be inclined to get a different lawyer!

Where the Bread Is Really Buttered

Not that Professional Courtesy operates only in the realm of scheduling. In fact, it is a consideration that enters into every nook of legal practice.

Now, it should be understood that lawyers are ethically bound to pursue their clients' interests with all due diligence, and to steer clear of any conflicting claims on their professional loyalties. All reputable attorneys treat that fiduciary responsibility with the highest respect; and of course clients have recourse to malpractice suits or complaints to local bar associations if they feel their lawyers have in any way breached their trust.

For all that, however, lawyers have a broad range of discretion as to how they can behave in a given situation.

A lawyer can be less aggressive or more aggressive, cooperative or belligerent.

In a contract negotiation, a lawyer can be flexible or intransigent; in a dispute, he can lean towards settlement or towards pitched battle.

A lawyer can make the other side's attorney look good or look bad, appear reasonable and fair or the soul of villainy.

And every client should be aware that those choices have to do, in part, with the sort of relationship that the lawyer has, or has had, or would like to have, with the other side's attorneys.

In every business, after all, one's colleagues and competitors are as important as one's customers.

The Dynamic of the Two-lawyer Town

Say that you and I are the only two lawyers in a sleepy little town in Arkansas. Let's analyze the professional relationship between the two of us.

First and foremost, we are competitors. We compete for clients, we compete for reputation, we both want to be known as the smartest legal eagle in town.

On the other hand, we really can't afford to be enemies. Chances are we'll be on the phone with each other three, four

47

times a week, every week of our working lives. We will be trying to expedite settlements which, aside from benefiting our clients, will free us to take on other business and make more money. Now and then you'll be booked solid and you'll send clients my way; now and then I'll do the same for you.

Clients will come and go; magistrates will come and go; but you and I will still be there, the only two entries in the local directory under Lawyers.

So I don't want you mad at me.

If a prospective client comes to me and wants to know why he should hire me as opposed to you, I'll do my sell job, but I will think twice before I say anything negative about you. (If I want the business bad enough, however, making you look terrible will probably be easy, as we shall shortly discuss.)

If we show up before a judge one day, and it turns out you haven't done your homework, I'll stop short of humiliating you because I don't want you waiting for an opportunity to embarrass me in return.

If we're due at a hearing at 9.00 a.m. and you call me at eight to ask for an adjournment, I will give it to you because next time it might be *my* kid who has 'flu and keeps me up all night.

Again, these courtesies that you and I extend to each other should not substantively affect the results of the services we provide. Still, politeness costs time and money – *clients'* time and money.

Your customers and my customers are picking up the tab for our mutual graciousness. And let's face it – it's easy to be gracious when someone else is paying.

The Hidden Costs

Everybody complains about legal fees. Not everybody thinks about the *hidden* costs that are incurred when lawyers, practising professional courtesy, do not take the shortest path between points A and B.

Some years ago, a woman of my acquaintance had to bivouac at the Carlyle Hotel for three weeks, at around $200 a night, because *her estranged husband's lawyer* was on vacation and her own attorney felt it would be improper to file divorce papers before he was back.

Another time, our company was negotiating an endorsement deal for French skier Jean-Claude Killy. Killy was to be paid in dollars, but the number of dollars was pegged to the dollar's value relative to the franc.

Well, midway through the contract process, the other side's attorney had to fly to Milan to tend to another matter altogether. Our lawyers, rather than insisting that the Killy business be passed along to another attorney so that it could be resolved in a timely manner, agreed to wait until the first fellow returned from Italy. Meanwhile, the franc went on a short-term spree that lowered the value of Killy's deal by around 6 per cent.

Now, they don't teach you about currency fluctuations at law school, and that 6 per cent won't show up on anybody's legal bills – but what is it, if not part of the cost of dealing with lawyers?

Meanwhile, Back at the Ranch . . .

But coming back to the example of the two lawyer town – I realize that situation is an extreme one, but I use it for a very simple reason. In any location in any area of law, and at any level of prestige and clout, the dynamics that obtain among attorneys are essentially the dynamics of the small town.

Whether you're talking about sole practitioners who do criminal work in Brooklyn, or three-hundred-lawyer firms engaged in billion-dollar antitrust suits, the number of players in any given arena is finite.

'What goes 'round, comes 'round', as the saying goes, and if lawyers do business once, chances are they'll do business again. Unless they are saints or fools, protecting their ongoing relationships with fellow attorneys will be part of their agenda. No client should be so naive as not to realize that.

Insofar as it's possible to do so, therefore, clients should always try to learn about the history of the relationship between the lawyer they themselves intend to hire, and the attorney or firm retained by the other side.

How can you do this? In the simplest way imaginable: ask.

Ask your lawyer if he or she has dealt with the other side before.

Ask if those dealings have been friendly or hostile.

Ask if there are grudges or outstanding scores to settle.

Ask if there is any factor that might prevent your lawyer from serving your interests wholeheartedly and without complications.

In this, as in other aspects of dealing with lawyers, I cannot urge you too strongly to keep these two simple precepts in mind:

> It is always to the client's advantage to show sophistication by knowing the pertinent questions.
>
> Showing awareness *up front* is a great deterrent to being taken advantage of later on.

If you're embarking upon a hostile procedure that will call for snarling, threats and stonewalling, don't hire the other guy's brother-in-law or good old mate from school.

Conversely, for a matter that requires tact and cooperation, don't align yourself with an attorney who has a twenty-year grudge against his opposite number.

McCormack's Axiom of Showmanship

Lawyers, like vaudevillians, play as much to each other as to the audience.

How Lawyers Make Other Lawyers Look Bad

Not so very long ago, professional tennis was a fledgling enterprise that consisted largely of barnstorming pros who put on exhibitions, not for fat purses put up by corporate sponsors, but for only a percentage of the gate.

The nonpareil among those barnstormers was the great Australian lefty Rod Laver, who happened to be one of our

50

earliest tennis clients, and whose long career spanned the eras of barnstorming and big sponsorship.

One day I asked Laver how it was that in even-split exhibitions, he always made his opponents look so darn good and just barely edged them out; whereas in winner-take-all matches, it couldn't have been clearer that he had them all outclassed.

What Laver told me was that he truly wasn't conscious of hitting the ball any differently in either case. It was just that when there was money on the table, he mysteriously became a different sort of player.

I mention this story because it suggests an analogy to the behaviour of many lawyers: as long as lawyers are in a situation where both sides will benefit from making each other look good, they'll bend over backwards to do so.

When fees and clients are up for grabs, however, and one lawyer or firm is out to steal business from another, all bets are off as far as professional courtesy is concerned. The idea in these instances is to impugn the quality of the other lawyer's work – and no matter how solid that work really is, it can always be impugned.

'Fourscore and Seven Years Ago . . .'

I can still recall my eighth-grade history teacher who made us memorize the Gettysburg Address. As far as this teacher was concerned, the Gettysburg Address was the greatest document of all time – stirring, elegant, heroic.

Years later, I read an article about a college English professor who approached the Gettysburg Address as he would a freshman composition, and gave it a C minus! This article included references to Lincoln's mistakes in grammar and lapses in logic, and made a quite persuasive case that the speech was nothing special after all.

So if the Gettysburg Address can rate a C minus, imagine what the run-of-the-mill contract or legal memo would rate in the hands of someone with a vested interest in being a hard marker!

Lawyer Smith and Lawyer Jones

Lawyers don't simply welcome the opportunity to review the work of a competing attorney, they wallow in it.

Let's say that I am a lawyer named Smith and you are a client currently being represented by a lawyer named Jones. On some pretext or other, you call me up and ask to talk to me.

Now, before a word has been said, I'm at a strategic advantage: obviously you're having some qualms about the service you're getting from Jones, or you wouldn't be consulting me.

You come up to my office (which is decorated in such a way as to inspire total confidence, of course), and I make it a point to be extra attentive and totally sympathetic. I go into what I think of as my 'audition mode' — which is probably more impressive than Jones's usual behaviour simply because it's more impressive than *my* usual behaviour; it's our first date, after all.

Now, if you are a typical client, you will probably avoid saying anything overtly bad about Jones, because ironically you'll be concerned about insulting *me* by insulting a member of my profession. So we'll do a delicate little dance around the subject of your not being happy with Jones. The dance will go something like this:

> You say: I'm involved in a very important matter and I want to make sure I understand what's going on.
>
> (You mean: I'm terrified that this procedure is going to take me to the cleaners and I'm desperately in need of reassurance.)
>
> I say: In any matter of this sort, it's very important that you have total faith in the person representing you.
>
> (I mean: I know you're nervous about Jones and I want to make you so nervous that you won't be able to stand one more day with him as your attorney.)
>
> You say: It's not that I don't have faith in Mr Jones . . .

(You mean: It *is* that I don't have faith in Mr Jones.)

I say: Sometimes these things are just a matter of personal chemistry.

(I mean: You don't have to feel guilty if you think this guy's a jerk.)

You say (meekly): Well, I wonder if I might just ask you a question or two.

(You mean: Save me!)

I say: I can't advise you while you're being represented by someone else, but if there's some specific document . . .

(I mean: Let me get my hands on something Jones has written, so I can gleefully tear it to shreds.)

What, No Framastam Clause?!

Let's suppose that you have brought along a contract that Jones has drafted for you. You hand it to me across the desk, and now the real fun begins.

I peruse the document and, without looking up, I am perfectly aware that you are scrutinizing my expression, looking for any sign of disapproval. If I so much as raise an eyebrow, you will probably think, 'Oh my God, what is this clown Jones doing to me?'

If I murmur something to the effect of 'Odd that he didn't put a choice of laws clause in here,' you'll probably go through agonies wondering what *else* he hasn't put in.

And if, after going through three or four pages, I say, 'Now, here's something I would have done differently,' chances are you'll find yourself wishing that the whole thing had been in my hands to begin with.

Maybe I win you over as a client. At the very least, I've exacerbated the doubts you already have about Jones. But here's the thing that most clients would probably not realize.

In the whole mini-drama that you and I have just played out, there has been *not one solitary scrap of evidence that I, in fact, could represent you better than, or even necessarily as well as, Jones.*

Maybe I have made you *feel* I could – but that's an emotional response, not one based on anything that has actually been demonstrated.

Poor Jones hasn't been around to defend himself or state his case. If the situation had been reversed, and Jones was looking at a contract that *I* had drawn up, he could have nitpicked every bit as effectively as I did.

Not that my contract would have been flawed, any more than *his* was necessarily flawed; it's just that there are virtually infinite ways to draw up a document, and a lawyer can always say, or suggest, that his own way is superior.

So What's a Client To Do?

This state of affairs, as should be clear, leaves clients with a dilemma. Given that any competent lawyer can call into question the quality of another lawyer's work, how *should* a client know which attorney to stay with – or, for that matter, to do business with in the first place?

The terrible truth is that there are no hard-and-fast rules about this. If there were, the best lawyers would get all the business, and the rest would get none at all – and anyone with eyes in his head knows that isn't true. In general, however, I would suggest the following bits of practical advice:

– Appraise a lawyer *not* by what he says about other lawyers' efforts, but on the basis of *positive* statements of what he himself would do for you.

– Don't base the choice of attorney *solely* on the first impression he makes on you, but don't disregard that factor, either. If he impresses you, he'll probably impress colleagues, judges and juries as well.

– Whenever possible, ask around about a lawyer's reputation. Talk to other clients who have employed him. One of the few things a smart lawyer can't conveniently misrepresent is what other people think of him.

How Lawyers Make Other Lawyers Look Good

If competing attorneys sometimes have obvious motivations for denigrating each other's work, *opposing* attorneys sometimes have just slightly less apparent reasons for praising each other to the skies. Let me illustrate this by way of an example.

A few years ago, IMG was forced, on behalf of tennis star Mats Wilander, to sue a foreign clothing manufacturer for nonpayment of royalties that were approaching the million-dollar mark. The case, unfortunately for us, had to be tried in a jurisdiction in which we had no previous litigation experience. We hired local counsel, of course – a firm we had not dealt with before, but which had come to us very highly recommended.

Early on in the preparation of the case, we noticed a somewhat odd pattern emerging. In all their correspondence with us, the lawyers of the firm we had engaged seemed to be straining to say nice things about the *other side's* attorneys: they were so brilliant; they were so thorough; they were so well connected, so discreet, so resourceful.

Our lawyers made *their* lawyers sound so good, we kicked ourselves for not retaining them before our adversary did!

For a brief time, we tried to deny the truth of what was really going on. In multinational dealings, it is always a mistake to jump to conclusions; maybe this excessive colleagial generosity was simply their version of such conventions (almost always insincere!) as calling one's opposite number 'My esteemed colleague'.

After several months and some tens of thousands of dollars in legal fees had slipped away, however, the simple facts became clear. Our lawyers didn't believe we could win the case, and they were already taking steps to avoid or minimize the blame for losing it.

The right was unquestionably on our side, but for technical reasons peculiar to this jurisdiction, the outcome was not likely to be in our favour, and payment of the award would probably be impossible even if it did.

But our hired counsel, of course, hoped to do business with

us again. So their idea in praising the opposition so highly was to make us believe that in this particular case they had laboured heroically but tragically against incalculable odds, but that in any other battle they would surely prevail.

Since we take our battles one at a time, we were not unduly impressed.

The David-and-Goliath Trick

The ploy of building up the opposing lawyers is not used only to make a loss seem less embarrassing. If anything, the tactic is even more appealing to a lawyer who expects to win.

Excessive modesty is not something they teach you at law school. Still, a lawyer can't very well go around telling people how brilliant and eloquent he is, how he hypnotizes juries and so overwhelms judges with his exhaustive knowledge that they'll let him do whatever he wants.

If, however, he says all those things about his *opponent* – if he presents his opposite number as a judicial Goliath – and then goes on to beat him – well, the client will be free to draw his own conclusions.

Some years ago, IMG was put through a David-and-Goliath scenario on a matter that is rather comical in its sheer pettiness. During the same years our client Bjorn Borg was ruling men's tennis, the nation of Uruguay was going crazy over the sport. The Uruguayans had an apparently unslakable thirst for products – T-shirts, coffee mugs, beach towels – with Borg's name and likeness on them.

The only problem was, no one in Uruguay seemed inclined to take the time or trouble to license that name and image, or to look into the inconvenient fact of international trademarks and copyrights. The abuses were so flagrant that we had no choice but to hire a Uruguayan lawyer to try to straighten out the mess.

This lawyer was a character. He had an incredibly high-flown way of talking and writing, and from the start he made it sound as if the entire legal apparatus of Latin America was mobilized against him, and him alone. The fight would be long, hard and bitter, he warned us. Perhaps he could carry the day, but it would require every scrap of his wit and passion, because the other side was so crafty and so determined.

Forget that this was as clear-cut a case of infringement as could possibly be imagined, and a puny one at that! This fellow insisted on presenting it as a battle royal among the best legal minds of the age.

Eventually, we won the case – and our attorney sent us a bill that was roughly equivalent to two years' worth of the royalties we would see from the new licensing agreements.

At the end of that two years, by the way, the Uruguayan tennis craze was pretty well played out, and that was the end of the Borg beach-towel fad!

So I would say, watch out if your attorney has too many nice things to say about the opposing lawyers. Chances are, one way or the other, his adulation is going to cost you money.

Law Firm Economics 101

Of all the sorts of information that lawyers don't particularly like to share with laymen, facts and figures on law firm economics come high on the list.

Hundreds of thousands of dollars are spent on research studies on the subject, but the results are virtually never circulated outside the profession.

Why?

Maybe lawyers are concerned that the general public will resent them even more than it already does, if people find out, for example, that:

– Median *after-tax* income for partners of large American law firms is closing in on the $250,000 mark. Reckoning by median minimizes the impact of partners' compensation at the very top firms, where annual incomes are often in the seven-figure range.

– Many people, myself included, are outraged by the run-away judgments routinely awarded these days in American liability cases. But do you know how much of every judgment actually ends up going to the plaintiffs? *Thirty-seven cents of every dollar awarded.* The rest is gobbled up in legal fees and expenses.

– In the typical instance, law firms shell out roughly $65,000 per lawyer per year for rent and other operating expenses – meaning, of course, that clients foot the bill for that egregious overhead *before* an attorney does one single thing on their behalf.

– In spite of this whopping overhead, law firms operate at an average profit margin of 42 per cent. For most businesses, a margin of 10 per cent is comfortable, and 20 per cent is considered excellent. But then, a law firm is a different kind of store.

Cracking the Nut

Meeting the overhead is, of course, the first item on a lawyer's economic agenda.

No client should overlook the role played by operating expenses in determining what his legal costs will be. No client should kid himself about who pays for the signed prints on the wall, the teak desks, the creamy stationery.

As evidence of just how crucial overhead is, consider this tale.

Recently, one of our broadcasting clients was in the process of simultaneously selling a Manhattan co-op and buying a house in a quiet little town on the east end of Long Island.

A house closing is considerably more complicated than a co-op closing; there are title searches and surveys to be done, on-premises inspections, and so forth. Further, the lawyer's role on behalf of a seller is almost always less complicated than on behalf of a buyer. Finally, the price tag on the house was just more than double the apartment's.

For all that, legal fees on the co-op closing were *four times greater* than on the house purchase.

Why?

Because the attorney on the house closing was a local fellow who had a perfectly decent office above a hardware store on

Main Street, and the attorney on the co-op closing had a suite on a high floor in a building in Madison Avenue.

Both lawyers gave competent service in what were, after all, totally routine procedures.

This fellow didn't *need* a fancy lawyer for the apartment transaction any more than he needed his Rolls-Royce to drive to the corner for a pint of milk. But this leads me to give the following warning:

McCormack's Axiom of Location, Location and Location

If you insist on doing business in an expensive neighbourhood, you're going to end up paying your lawyer's exorbitant rent.

How Do You Spell Chutzpah?

In most businesses there are limits as to how much overhead can be passed along to consumers. Lawyers have succeeded in pushing that threshold almost to infinity.

The bottom line is that *unless you ride shotgun on them, lawyers will charge you pretty much whatever they want for whatever level of service they feel like providing.*

There's a great story about a man named Ben Sonnenberg, who was one of the inventors of modern public relations as well as one of the greatest self-promoters of all time. Back in 1958, when the Ford Motor Company decided to close up shop on the disastrous Edsel, company executives were frantic about the long-term damage being done to corporate prestige.

They went to Sonnenberg and asked his advice on the best way to restore the patina on the company name.

Sonnenberg told them that, for $50,000, he would think about the problem and bestow upon them the benefit of his wisdom. Ford forked over the cash, and Sonnenberg went home to ponder. A week later, he told them, 'Do nothing.'

That's what Ford got for its fifty thousand.

I mention this story because while lawyers' fees are seldom

59

quite so unconscionable on a piecework basis, their method of charging has several things in common with Mr Sonnenberg's.

– Typically, a lawyer simply names his price and the client has no choice but to take it or leave it.

– Except in contingency-fee cases, the client pays dearly regardless of result.

– *The practitioner bills virtually without accountability*, and does so in a climate where there is almost no standard for judging whether his price is fair.

Monitoring the Meter

Are there ways to make lawyers more accountable in their billing?

The answer is yes and no.

A client should always demand a complete and detailed bill from his attorney, and should review the document carefully.

Ideally, the bill should be issued *monthly* – before fees can get too far out of control.

It should reflect the charges and contributions of everyone – paralegals, secretaries and so on – working on your case.

It should include all items like telephone bills, photocopying, messengers.

A lawyer's bill, in short, should be as airtight as the receipt you get from the supermarket.

The Illusion of Precision

That said, however, the terrible truth remains: *reviewing* a lawyer's charges is not the same thing as being able to *control* a lawyer's charges.

It is still in the lawyer's sole discretion, for example, to bill a full quarter-hour 'unit' if he leaves a thirty-second message on someone's answering machine.

A lawyer may still bill you full rate for the five hours he sits on an aeroplane on your behalf – and you have no way of knowing if *another* client's file was on his lap during the flight, and if *that* client is being billed as well.

Even in a detailed accounting, there will be places to hide such oddments as (this is a true story!) the dry-cleaning bills of paralegals who see business trips as opportunities to have their entire wardrobes cleaned by the hotel valet service.

As ever, then, in the war between clients and lawyers, the lawyers have a broad range of tactical advantages on their side. Still, there are moves that clients can make to give themselves a fighting chance – and in the chapter that follows, we'll talk about some nuts-and-bolts prescriptions for evening up the odds.

4

A Primer for Clients

There's an old quip about the businessman who is asked by a colleague to recommend a good lawyer.

'I can't,' the fellow says, 'because there aren't any. There are only *effective* lawyers – and, come to think of it, I can't come up with many of those either.'

Turning the joke around, the same thing could be said of clients.

There are effective clients and ineffective clients; clients who promote their own best interests and clients who shoot themselves in the foot; clients who save themselves money on legal fees and clients who unwittingly conspire in running up their bills.

How and why do some clients make their lives even more miserable than necessary when dealing with law-yers?

Usually it comes down to not knowing the right questions to ask. Or being afraid to ask those questions. Or failing to understand the answers.

It's understandable that these difficulties might affect clients who have recourse to lawyers only a few times in their lives. Less understandable is the fact that even sophisticated clients are often hamstrung by the same uncertainties and lack of self-assertion.

Why?

Basically, because lawyers – not all, but many – are happy to preserve an aura of mystery and their stance of subtle intimidation.

They aren't taught that stance in law school, you understand. But, boy, do they ever learn that it comes in handy in real life!

Not Just Another Pretty Face

Many clients make things worse for themselves by the sheer lack of thought with which they choose an attorney in the first place.

They hire someone because they have a passing acquaintance with him at the squash club.

Or because he once represented their brother-in-law in some entirely different sort of procedure.

Or because his office is convenient to where they have their poodle groomed.

Most of IMG's clients have personal attorneys, and while I obviously can't name names in this connection, I have sometimes been appalled at their choices.

We have had boxing clients who apparently picked lawyers because they were fight buffs; these attorneys might *literally* have been good to have in your corner, but you wouldn't want them standing between you and the legal system.

Similarly, we have had skiing clients who apparently chose lawyers because they would be comfortable meeting them on the slopes.

It is human nature, I suppose, to want to do business with people who share in your passions and who flatter your vanity by being your fans. But this is no way to pick an attorney; and in fact it leads me to propose another rule.

McCormack's Hardnosed Axiom of Lawyer Selection

Hire the person who can do the job – and accept that the person who can do the job isn't necessarily the person you want to be best friends with.

Keep in mind, too, that the right lawyer for one job may not be the right lawyer for *every* job.

A fresh-scrubbed, horn-rimmed Ivy Leaguer might be just

63

the fellow to ease you through a deal with an investment bank, but chances are he would get eaten alive in a battle with an inner-city DA.

A gritty sole practitioner might do just fine in a toe-to-toe with the DA, but wouldn't win you points with the investment bank.

You don't have to know one single thing about the law itself to be able to make these judgments. You just have to pay attention.

Ask and Ye Won't Be Taken

But again, paying *effective* attention is easier said than done.

Most people who fail to get themselves the right lawyer do so for one of three reasons:

— Either they're too lazy to make inquiries or shop around, even though in most cities three or four well-placed phone calls will get them all the information they need.

— Or they're so insecure that they don't believe they can judge a lawyer's competence.

— Or they're so misguidedly impressed with lawyers that they assume that since Mr X or Ms Y has been called to the bar, he or she must have a handle on every entry in the legal lexicon.

This, if you think about it even for a moment, is a bizarre assumption. In fact, there is no one on earth who knows all the law.

There is no one who knows half the law, and I would venture to say that a person with a real, intimate working knowledge of even one thousandth of the law has a claim to be thought of as a giant of jurisprudence!

The law has become a profession of specialist areas with each area getting more fine-tuned every day. It is therefore more crucial than ever to *find a lawyer whose technical abilities suit your present needs.*

Don't be afraid to ask a lawyer head on if he or she has expertise in a particular matter.

64

Don't be afraid to ask if he or she has handled similar cases before.

Ask for specific examples.

Lawyers, like the rest of us, enjoy a new challenge and welcome the opportunity to expand their professional repertoire. If you don't *force* them to go on the record with an accounting of their experience, chances are they'll keep mum on the subject of their *in*experience.

Remember: you're not shelling out good money for the privilege of being a guinea pig.

Don't put yourself on the line so that the *next* person can have the benefit of an experienced attorney

Home Court Advantage

Just as different lawyers stake out different areas within the law, they stake out different geographical turfs, too; and usually it is to a client's advantage to have local representation.

There are several reasons for this. One, especially in smaller cities and towns, there tends to be a prejudice against the 'city slickers' and a bias in favour of the native sons or daughters. It is also true that local counsel, generally speaking, will be better able to monitor a given situation, especially if that situation is susceptible to changes in the political or economic climate in their particular area.

Let me give a few examples that underline the importance of being 'turf-sensitive' where legal matters are concerned.

A WIN IN PITTSBURGH

IMG was involved in a major legal action concerning a professional sports team in Pittsburgh, and we were debating what sort of firm we should hire to represent us.

The matter was a complicated one and the stakes were high, and my first impulse — call it a prejudice, if you like — was to retain one of the most high-powered New York firms.

Before taking this step, however, we spoke with a partner of one of Pittsburgh's leading outfits, who gave us an account of a horrendous experience *he* had had when trying a case in North Carolina. The judge and the opposing lawyers had known each other for years, and everything that happened in the courtroom made him feel not just that he was from another state, but from another planet.

The implication was plain enough: although they don't teach it this way at law school, the rules of impartiality always have enough slack in them to give an edge to the home team.

This attorney suggested that, while Pittsburgh wasn't small-town North Carolina, we would still be better off aligning ourselves with a firm that was familiar with Pittsburgh judges, Pittsburgh clerks, and 'the Pittsburgh way of getting things done'.

We were persuaded to retain him, and in fact the hometown nature of the resulting legal work was more than satisfactory.

A DISASTER DOWN UNDER

To illustrate what can happen when a client *isn't* sensitive to the question of a lawyer's turf, I must pass along an account of perhaps the costliest tactical error I ever made in the selection of an attorney.

A number of years ago, I and a group of IMG clients invested in a leasehold on 1.2 million acres in the Northern Territory of Australia, not far from the town of Darwin. This parcel of land was almost the size of Holland, and we leased it long-term for less than a dollar an acre.

The government of Australia was the lessor on the property; its goal, of course, was to promote the development of the Northern Territory. Accordingly, the government wrote a provision in the lease stating that the land had to be improved by a certain amount of investment each year, for the building of fences and so forth, so that the property could be used for cattle.

Now, we had no intention of getting into the ranching business. We had bought the property as a speculation – and had made this very clear to the prestigious Sydney-based lawyer who handled the transaction for us. The lawyer, in turn, assured us that we had nothing to worry about. No one had ever paid any attention to the land-improvement clauses. They were in the nature of a mere formality, and no one ever inspected the property.

Besides, would anyone really insist that we build a fence around a piece of property almost the size of Holland?

As it happened, someone would.

Shortly after we acquired the lease, a man named Gough Whitlam became prime minister of Australia. He had run his campaign on an Australia First theme, and one of his promises was to discourage foreign investment and foreign ownership of Australian property and assets.

This was going on half a world away from where we were based, you understand, and with all due respect to the importance of Australia's domestic politics, Mr Whitlam's sentiments were not exactly making world news. We were dependent on Our Man in Sydney to keep us posted.

But here we had made a terrible misjudgement. Sydney is about as far from the Northern Territory as, say, New York is from Nevada, and, as the saying goes, all politics is local politics. Our cosmopolitan attorney simply didn't understand how virulent (and how opportunistic) was the nationalist feeling in the frontier north.

So it took us absolutely by surprise when we were suddenly informed that our Holland-sized piece of land had reverted to the state because of our failure to develop it! We were given no warning of this turn of events, and no chance to correct the situation. It was just handed to us as a *fait accompli.*

Eventually we went to court in northern Australia and, after great trouble and expense, managed to reach a reasonable settlement with the government.

But matters should never have come to that. All along, we would have been better served by a sole practitioner in a dusty office in the northern boondocks – someone who *knew the turf and was in a position to sense the changing climate* – than by our fancy lawyer who was hopelessly out of touch with the local realities.

Before leaving the subject of geographical leverage, I would like to relate another anecdote that has a happier note. A good friend of mine charters a yacht each summer in the Greek islands for a month. This friend happens to be one of the world's leading experts in the laws of admiralty and shipping, and someone who is intimately acquainted with the Greek courts.

One day, while my friend was happily sailing along with his family, the owner of the yacht called the ship's captain on the radio and informed him that he needed the boat for his own use. The owner ordered the captain to get my friend and his family to disembark at the nearest port. The captain was quite embarrassed, but passed along this unfortunate message on behalf of his employer, the shipowner. The unfortunate owner, of course, had no idea what he was getting involved in.

Within three days, my friend had filed a suit for harassment and damages in the courts of Corfu, had been awarded several thousand dollars, and ultimately ended up getting a luxury cruise in the Greek islands for nothing, as well as the money.

It pays to know the local customs.

Style As Well As Substance

Not long ago, a writer friend called me for advice about changing literary agents.

She had just signed a contract for her second book, and was receiving an advance more than double the amount she had received for her first.

She was being paid top dollar and was often getting cover credits from several major magazines.

In all, her career was going swimmingly, and I asked her why in the world she was thinking of dropping her agent.

'Because he embarrasses me,' she said. 'He's got this fast-talking, Hollywood style, and when I meet editors he's dealt with, I often feel that the first thing I have to let them know is that I'm not like him.'

Her story really hit home, because I still have a very sharp recollection of the first time I was made to realize **the importance of personal style in maintaining a business relationship.**

Back in my earliest days of representing athletes, I was at a beach club in Santa Monica with Arnold Palmer. We were standing at the service counter, waiting to be given towels. For no good reason, the simple process of getting the towels and having our changing facilities arranged turned out to be slow, complicated and annoying.

In those days, I was very aggressive, impatient and apt to be abrasive and sarcastic. I let it be known – to the checkout clerk himself and to everyone within earshot – that I thought he was a bit of an idiot.

I was nasty, but I was right.

Later on, in private, Arnold gave me a more than stern talking-to. He didn't treat people that way, and he didn't want those associated with him treating people that way.

He felt it was a reflection on him – and he was right. Ever since then, whenever I do anything with or on behalf of a client, I keep in mind that the top priority is not how *I'll* feel about it but how *the client* will feel.

With lawyers as well as with agents, personal style matters deeply, and there's no sense hiring someone who has the technical ability but who sets your teeth on edge.

Clearly, if you're hiring an attorney to represent you in a hostile procedure in which everybody hates everybody and you'll never do business again, you may as well get the toughest, gruffest bulldog you can find. As the saying goes, *'If you're hiring a gun, get one that can shoot'*.

Often, however, your lawyer will be representing you vis-à-vis people you'll be dealing with in the future.

If he is sleazy, you'll be sleazy by association.

If he's intractable on a given issue, chances are you will run into intractability from the other side somewhere down the road.

So try to find someone whose approach is consonant with your own. But, as I said earlier, the idea is not to be sentimental

or to pick a lawyer because he's a friend. That's a mistake.
Keep in mind this rule of thumb:

McCormack's Axiom of Association

If you're not comfortable with the idea that someone might *think* the lawyer is a friend of yours, then
you probably shouldn't do business.

Avoid the Quick Dissatisfiers

If you hire an attorney to represent you in a lawsuit, and the
lawsuit takes two years to conclude or reach a settlement, it
will probably take you the same two years to decide finally
whether or not you were happy with the lawyer's services: in
the end, it's results that matter.

Along the way, however, there will probably be hundreds
of small details in which the lawyer will satisfy or frustrate
you, win your confidence or make you angry.

Does he return your phone calls?

Does he explain things to you in a manner you can understand?

Does he make an effort to be available when *you* are?

Does he keep you posted about important developments in
the case, or does he leave you in the dark?

These are the kinds of issues I think of as the potential quick
dissatisfiers – and *avoiding them is the client's responsibility as
much as the attorney's.*

Different clients have different needs – emotional as well
as practical. And a great deal of trouble and ill feeling can be
avoided if a client is clear and explicit about his needs from
the beginning.

Are you the type of person who requires a fair amount of
hand-holding?

If so, ask your lawyer if you would be able to reach him,
if need be, in the evenings or on weekends. Ask him if he
tends to be away for weeks at a time, and how his office is
covered when he's gone.

70

Do you get paranoid if you feel you're losing control of things?

If so, you should make a point of asking to be kept abreast of all procedures, copies of letters and memos, etc.

If, on the other hand, you're happier not being bothered with details, tell your lawyer you want to be shielded from them, and that you want to hear nothing from him except when to appear in court.

For your own peace of mind, let your attorney know where you stand on these basic contact and involvement issues. And make sure he's willing to do things the way you want them done.

Remember, when you're the client you're the boss, even if sometimes it doesn't feel that way.

Your lawyer should be accountable to you in whatever reasonable form you are comfortable with.

How Smart in Business Should a Business Lawyer Be?

The crux of being an effective client lies in knowing how to get a lawyer to give you the service you need.

But there is another side of it as well. **knowing how to prevent a lawyer from meddling in situations where 'the legal approach' just isn't appropriate.**

Giving credit where credit is due, most lawyers are pretty intelligent people.

They have the analytical tools to go after a problem, and they are generally quick studies of the specific requirements, customs and jargon of a given field.

However, the nature of their intelligence tends not to be the same as that of the more intuitive, improvising resourcefulness of the business person.

And when lawyers try too hard to apply their smarts to issues that are really *business* issues, the terrible truth is that they sometimes end up seeming not so smart at all.

In situations like that, *it is the client's responsibility to let the attorney know when to back off.*

71

I have no shortage of examples of misguided legal zeal in action – examples that illustrate the value of client oversight.

To understand the cases that follow, however, you need to know just a little about the steps by which a deal is generally concluded at a company like IMG.

To put it very simply, first, one of our line executives negotiates the basic deal points with executives of the company contracting for our client's services. Working out the deal points is often a tremendously delicate process that can take months.

Once the deal points are agreed to in principle, several sets of lawyers become involved – and *that's* where it really gets complicated. IMG's legal department drafts a document reflecting the understanding reached by the executives. This draft goes both to the other company's lawyers *and* to our client's own attorneys.

Now, even if the draft is a perfectly good representation of the agreement, and even if the deal is an advantageous one for all concerned, there is a very good chance that some or all of the lawyers will at this point try to get *something extra*.

Why?

Because they have to feel they're serving *some* purpose, after all.

Thus, we end up with lawyers' inappropriate *after-the-fact* meddling in other people's hard-won deals.

This causes potential problems – and we, as savvy clients, have to make sure those potential problems don't become actual problems.

First of all, negotiations, like sharks, have to keep moving forward or they die. *Any time the forward momentum of a deal is stopped in order to rehash things that were supposedly settled, there's a real chance the deal will fall apart.*

Additionally, *bringing in new issues late in the game casts doubt on the good faith of what has gone before.*

If the new requests are legitimate, why weren't they mentioned sooner? And what's to prevent them from seeming

72

sneaky or unfair, like a final jab thrown after the bell has sounded?

'Yes, But Who Wants Pictures of Thirty-year-old Sneakers?'

Consider this apparently innocent 'something extra' sought by the lawyers of the All-England Club in regard to the club's standard licensing agreement for use of the name 'Wimbledon'.

Wimbledon is one of the magic words in sport, and the All-England Club, owner of the tournament, takes in enormous promotional revenues for allowing the name to be linked to everything from sportswear to soft drinks.

As is perfectly normal in this sort of licensing arrangement, licensees are given access to the tennis stadium to shoot advertising and promotional photographs. Typically, these photographs will be of items like a can of soft drink sitting in the umpire's chair, or of a model posing in the stands wearing a certain brand of sunglasses.

Well, a number of years ago, a lawyer for All-England came up with the notion that at the termination of a given licensing agreement, copyrights of all pictures taken by the licensee should revert to the club.

On the face of it, this seemed a harmless enough suggestion. But in fact it placed an unconscionable burden on the licensee. Expensive and unwieldy mechanisms would have to be designed to make sure that all photographs were filed and preserved – for decades, in many cases. Licensees would have to negotiate with individual photographers, making it clear that *they* couldn't retain the copyright.

Besides, since in virtually every case the photographs were product shots of what the licensee happened to be selling, what good could it possibly do the All-England club to have them? Who needed an out-of-date picture of tennis sneakers standing at the baseline?

Nevertheless, this lawyer kept insisting on the photograph-copyright clause being inserted into the standard licensing agreement.

And you know what? We haven't had it inserted in any executed contract yet! Every licensee insisted on having it crossed out, and they were usually annoyed that it had even been inserted. So what was the point?

A Warehouse Full of Blusher

The question of copyrights on photographs is small potatoes compared with the 'something extra' that Michael Jackson's lawyers tried to get on a deal they were negotiating with Max Factor.

Max Factor wanted to launch a major line of Michael Jackson fragrances and cosmetics, and the fees involved were stratospheric. But Jackson's lawyers weren't satisfied with money alone. They wanted a clause stating that if Max Factor defaulted *for any reason*, the company would instantly forfeit its right to sell any licensed products it had in inventory.

This provision was totally unworkable. Max Factor's inventory could conceivably run into the tens of millions of dollars, and no corporate counsel would allow his company to take on that sort of exposure.

Second, insofar as the clause was presumably intended to safeguard Jackson from an intentional reneging by Factor, it was reasonable in theory. In fact, however, the licensing agreement ran to sixty-five pages, and was so complicated that Factor could have been *technically* in default if – literally – a memo blew off someone's desk.

What Jackson's lawyers were asking, then, was for Factor to put a giant club in their hands, the better to clobber the company with later on! They damn nearly lost the entire deal.

A Rude But Vital Question

For similar reasons, I happen to believe that a client should give the following reply when a lawyer starts making suggestions on the *business* aspect of a deal:

WHO THE HELL ASKED YOU???

This is not to say that lawyers *never* come up with helpful and even brilliant suggestions. They do – and it will be my pleasure to relate some of those instances in their proper place.

In the typical case, however, when lawyers try to horn in on the business aspects of a deal, the practical result is usually confusion and wasted time.

Keep in mind the following axiom.

McCormack's Axiom of the Divison of Labour

Lawyers *formalize* the deal. They shouldn't *do* the deal.

Arguing with the Experts

This question of legal expertise versus business savvy raises a more general issue that every client should be aware of – the issue of questioning one's own hired experts.

The conventional wisdom, of course, is that if you're paying someone good money for supposedly expert advice, you should either follow the advice or fire the expert; those are the only two acceptable options.

Well, I believe that the conventional wisdom is dead wrong on that score.

The value of expert opinion – legal or otherwise – lies not in following it blindly and absolutely, but simply in having it available as *data*. In that form, it can be factored in with *other* data, including one's own intuition and experience.

In 1984, when *Time* magazine was forced to defend itself against a libel suit brought by the Israeli military leader Ariel Sharon, I had a discussion with *Time*'s managing editor, Ray Cave, which neatly underlined the truth of this advice.

Needless to say, *Time* had hired an absolutely topnotch battery of lawyers to defend it; these were men and women with an impressive knowledge of the libel laws and of First

Amendment protections – and they had no shortage of expert advice to dispense.

At the same time, Cave realized that no one was better equipped to offer insight into journalistic procedure and sound reporting practices than the editors and writers of *Time* – i.e., his own staff.

So in this instance, the client, Time, Inc., found itself with two different sets of experts who had divergent priorities and who approached almost every issue somewhat differently. Ignoring either group would have been folly, and the Time management had the good sense to realize that both cadres should have a hearing.

The result was spirited discussion, sometimes argument – and an overall defence that was more intelligent and persuasive than either gang could have formulated on their own.

Leave Your Ego at the Door

It should be said, however, that just as lawyers sometimes do their clients a disservice by meddling where they shouldn't, clients sometimes do *themselves* an injury by believing they are the final authority on everything.

This tendency usually goes by the name of pigheadedness, and it can be a very expensive habit.

It might make sense to argue with an expert who is holding forth on some intimate aspect of *your own business*; it makes less sense to compare brains with someone who is reading you chapter and verse on the quirks of the tax code.

To judge effectively where your own competence fades off into vulnerability, and where your own good ideas tail off into bluster, you've got to leave your ego at the door.

And that's an absolutely basic requirement of being an effective client.

Beware of Being Overlawyered

One of the truly terrible things about many Western legal systems is that *the lawyers themselves are given such broad discretion in determining the pace and complexity – i.e., the* cost — *of most procedures by which they make their living.*

Built into the systems are all sorts of incentives for lawyers to be slow, obscurantist, contentious, long-winded. Law school might deny it, but there is a most obvious temptation for lawyers to do more lawyering than really needs doing.

For a slightly comical example of overlawyering at its worst, consider these two versions of so-called grant clauses typically included in licensing contracts.

> Licensor hereby grants to Company the right to use Licensor's trademarks on and in connection with the advertisement, distribution and sale of athletic shoes and athletic shoes only.

The above wording is perfectly clear and legally watertight. Now here is what an overly zealous lawyer might add to it (and in fact *has* added to it, this example being from our files!):

> Use by Company of the Licensor trademark on products other than athletic shoes shall result in immediate termination of this agreement and the forfeiture by Company of its rights hereunder, including the right to dispose of any inventory bearing Licensor's trade marks. Company agrees that Licensor shall have the right to enforce this obligation by injunctive relief and Company hereby indemnifies Licensor for any and all costs, expenses, damages, claims and expenses, including attorneys' fees, for any breach by Company of the foregoing obligations.

Just what in the name of heaven is the second version all about? It adds virtually nothing of substance to the first simple clause.

One party to a contract can *always* seek relief if the other party violates the contract's provisions; that's why they call it a contract!

Damages can *always* be sought — again, by definition.

So the second version does nothing except keep the billing

meter running while the lawyer labours basic points of law that are implied in any contract anyway.

The result, however, isn't quite so innocent because the overwriting and the overlawyering have dramatically changed the whole *tone* of the argument. The second clause is an example of what lawyers call 'confrontational drafting'; I think of it as 'duelling word processors'.

Based on the second version, it would seem that the Licensor expects the worst from this relationship, mistrusts the Licensee, and is ready to file a lawsuit at the very first hint of justification.

Is this the impression that the Licensor would like to convey at the beginning of a *cooperative* arrangement, the object of which is for *both sides* to make money?

Obviously it isn't. And it is the client's responsibility to make sure that his lawyer's language accurately reflects not just the *letter* of a deal, but the *spirit* of it as well.

Obnoxious by Association

The damage of being overlawyered, then, goes beyond the mere fact of being overcharged. The real danger is that your intentions are misrepresented. If your lawyer is obnoxious, you're obnoxious by association.

In the worst case, deals fall through, much to the bafflement of the principals, because the lawyers got carried away by their own pugnacity.

In less dramatic instances, positions harden, resentments accrue, and proceedings take on an adversarial flavour when they don't have to.

And of course everyone ends up paying more than is really necessary.

So how can a client avoid being overlawyered?

— Make it very clear to your attorney *from the start* whether you expect difficulty or cooperation from the other side.

— If there is a reservoir of trust and goodwill between you and your opposite number, let your lawyer know that — and stress that you want the present business to add to that reservoir, not deplete it.

– Review your lawyer's letters and documents along the way, and if you don't think they are appropriate in tone, say so.

Lawyers, like Doberman pinschers, tend to think they were put on earth to act menacingly. They've been bred to assume that's what their masters *want*. *So let your lawyer know when you want him to snarl and when he should try purring.*

Love Me, Love My Staff

I can still recall the first time I was wooed by a New York law firm.

This was roughly two decades ago, when IMG was a far smaller company than it is today. Still, sports promotion was a tremendous growth industry at the time, athletes were achieving celebrity status more and more – and where there's money and visibility, there's litigation. So lawyers began to be interested in soliciting our business.

On this particular morning I went to the offices of a major midtown firm. I'd never been there before, but the receptionist, well briefed, knew my name before I told her. A secretary brought me freshly brewed coffee in an exquisite china cup. Then, without a moment's delay, I was ushered in to meet a senior partner – a man who wore the whitest shirt I have ever seen, before or since.

This gentleman impressed the hell out of me. On his office wall, there was a gallery of photographs of himself with various CEOs of major companies, and a couple of heads of state thrown in for good measure. He was a terrific storyteller, with real wit, charm, and a stash of anecdotes stretching back to encounters with FDR, Gary Cooper and Marlene Dietrich.

He took me to lunch at a place where it was famously difficult to get a table, where he was fawned on and personally visited by the chef. He ordered wine that had been in the bottle longer than I had been in long pants. In short, he was one of the worldliest and most magnetic men I had ever met in my life.

He was so charismatic that I almost didn't realize that *he would have virtually nothing to do with the sort of service I would or wouldn't get from his firm*!

He wouldn't be handling my cases. His elegant shoulders probably hadn't darkened the doorway of a courtroom in fifteen years. He was an ambassador – what is known in the trade as a 'rainmaker'. He brought in business by impressing, regaling, and tickling the vanity of youngish men such as I was at the time.

I tell this story because it suggests what I believe is a common mistake on the part of clients. Too often, a client pays too much attention to the image of a firm or to its figureheads, and too little attention to the younger attorneys, paralegals and functionaries *who actually service the account*.

A client should keep in mind that, in most instances, he or she is hiring not a single individual but a *team*. And the team is only as effective as its least effective member.

The most masterful trial work performed by a partner can be undermined if the associates and researchers haven't adequately prepared the case. A delicate negotiation being handled by a $500-an-hour lawyer can go down the tubes if a $40-an-hour paralegal has missed a deadline or got the facts wrong.

Beyond the Whitest Shirt

Clients, then, should ask at the outset **who at the firm will be responsible for what.**

Clients should not feel shy about asking to meet and interview others who will play a part in their case.

If personnel change, as often happens, during the course of a legal action, clients should be advised of the change; you don't want the second-string coming into the game at a crucial juncture.

Don't let the impressiveness of the person in the corner

office blind you to the necessity of having quality reflected *throughout* the firm you're dealing with.

This Little Matter of Money

One of the shrewder observations of human nature was made by a humorist named Kin Hubbard. 'When a man says it hain't the money but the principle o' the thing,' this fellow commented, 'it's th' money.'

So it tends to be with legal actions. And so it certainly tends to be with relationships between clients and lawyers. At law school they teach you that the best attorney is the one who gets the best grades; out in the world, most people consider the best attorney to be the one who rakes in the most lucre.

Lawyers are obviously concerned with how much money a given client or a given action will bring in to the coffers. Clients are just as obviously concerned with how much a given procedure is going to cost them, and whether, on balance, they will gain or lose by the time the thing is over.

For all that, clients and lawyers, in the typical instance, talk about fees and costs surprisingly little.

They don't talk about them soon enough, openly enough, with enough creativity, or in enough detail.

Why?

Because such discussions tend to make everyone uncomfortable, and clients therefore avoid them – usually to their cost.

The legal profession takes the quite explicit stance that **fees should be candidly discussed at the beginning of a relationship;** however, no one says the attorney has to be the one to initiate the discussion.

Usually that responsibility devolves upon the client; and usually the lawyer is just as happy if the client doesn't quite know how to broach the subject.

What, then, are the questions that a lawyer should be asked? Here's a brief list:

1. *What is your hourly rate, and what are the hourly rates of others who will be working on the case?*

This, of course, is an absolutely basic question. On the

81

other hand, it is one that clients get fixated on when they shouldn't.

If a lawyer tells you he charges $500 an hour and bills in quarter-hour segments, you'll probably swallow hard when you realize it's going to cost you *at least* $125 every time he lifts a pencil or a telephone on your behalf.

But if that lawyer is skilful enough to find a short cut so that a potentially drawn-out lawsuit is settled in a month, he is a bargain at his price.

Keep in mind, too, that top-ticket lawyers are charging you not just for *what* they know, but *who* they know.

A couple of years ago, a friend of mine was involved in a very delicate import-export matter that involved negotiations with the upper echelons of a foreign government. He hired an attorney who charged him $1000 per hour – but who was able to get a former vice-president of the United States to stand in as an intermediary in the discussions.

During my early days at Arter, Hadden, I recall a client being told that senior partners at the firm billed at a rate of $175 an hour – which was very much the high end of the market at the time. 'How fast do they work?' the client asked. The remark was facetious, but there's wisdom in it.

Hourly rates should be appraised with a full awareness that one lawyer's hour can be another lawyer's week, and that some lawyers can accomplish with a single phone call what others couldn't pull off in a lifetime!

2. *What about expenses?*

I will never forget the first time I saw a pack of lawyers gleefully squandering a client's money on limos, champagne and overpriced food at the most expensive restaurant they could find.

I was serving as co-counsel on this case; a glitzy New York firm provided the lead attorneys, who were in charge of handling expenses. For them it was all first-class air travel, de luxe hotels, and foie gras.

Frankly, I don't think they really enjoyed the luxuries they lavished on themselves. I think the fun just lay in the childish thrill of seeing how much they could get away with. They loved playing the big spenders — as long as it was with someone else's money.

I'm certainly not suggesting that that sort of decadent behaviour is typical of lawyers. The champagne-and-truffles banquet, however, neatly illustrates a point that every client should be aware of: the question of 'expenses' for legal work can cover a multitude of sins, and boundaries should be set as early on as possible.

If the work entails air travel, will the lawyers fly first class?

Will they stay at the priciest hotel in town or be content with something less grand?

Will there be a cap on expenses for meals?

Also, if a lawyer is travelling on your behalf, how many hours will he bill? Some lawyers may do two hours of work for you while travelling and bill you for eight, on the grounds that they *would* have worked eight if they were at their desk. By the same reasoning, some lawyers might bill *twelve* hours, claiming that's their normal workday.

Clients should understand that some lawyers — especially when working for a company presumed to have deep pockets — operate on the premise that they can get away with this sort of padding because their bills won't be closely scrutinized anyway.

A couple of years ago, I heard a terrific story that illustrates what a dramatic effect it can have when lawyers' bills *are* closely examined.

Company A and company B were engaged in a bitter and drawn-out lawsuit. The lawyers for company B wanted to settle, but the lawyers for company A refused: they were having too good a time, flying first class to Europe to take depositions in Geneva and Paris, lapping up caviar on the Concorde, and shopping for their wives and girl friends on the client's time. Obviously, the general counsel of company A had given them a long leash and was not watching the meter.

During the discovery phase of the lawsuit, however, the attorneys for company B pulled off a masterstroke. They managed to convince the judge that the billing records of company A's lawyers were germane to the case, and therefore should be handed over to be examined by all parties!

When the extravagant company of attorneys realized *everyone* would see the blatant evidence of all that chateaubriand and vintage Burgundy, they promptly agreed to settle.

Clearly, the abuses in this story were extreme. The fact is, however, that lawyers are generally not averse to spending their client's money. And keep this in mind:

McCormack's Axiom of Inverse Proportions

They'll spend more of it, the less the client seems to care.

So let your lawyer know you *do* care. Make it clear from the outset that you'll be reviewing all expenses, and that you expect your attorneys to be reasonable and prudent. By doing this, you'll save yourself some most unpleasant surprises when the bills come in.

3. *Is there a retainer, and if so, what does it cover?*
Some lawyers – in a practice that is analogous to charging admission to a department store – charge clients a 'retainer' merely for opening up a file in their name.

Other firms charge a retainer that is essentially a guarantee of a certain amount of billed time per month or quarter, and against which actual billed time is credited.

Other firms charge no retainer at all.

Find out from the start how a prospective lawyer handles this issue. If there is a retainer, ask how it is justified; if nothing else, it is highly entertaining to note the ingenuity with which attorneys answer this question.

4. *Is there a contingent-fee arrangement?*
As I have said before and will say again, I believe that the contingency-fee system, as it applies to liability cases, is one of the things that is disastrously, catastrophically wrong with the American legal system.

In *some* instances, however, hiring a lawyer on a pay-for-results basis makes sense for all concerned – for the client, for the attorney, and for that vague entity known as the common good.

If, for example, one of IMG's clients is in a position to file a suit for unpaid royalties, it might make sense to pay the lawyers not an hourly fee, but a percentage of monies collected, regardless of how much time or work it takes. This creates an incentive to get the matter resolved expediently and a *dis*incentive to drag it out; in most cases, it leads to an out-of-court settlement that allows one more trial to vanish from the docket.

There are certain issues a client should address in *any* sort of contingent-fee arrangement:

> What will be the lawyer's percentage of the take?
> What sorts of costs and expenses will come off the top, *before* the pot is divvied up?
> Who will bear what part of those costs and expenses if you lose?

Don't assume that a contingency agreement means you have a free ride until the award comes rolling in. Award or no, the terrible truth is that you'll almost always find a bill is in the post.

Also, there's no law stating that a lawyer-client relationship must run on either a straight hourly rate or a straight contingency basis.

Everything is negotiable – though this is one of the things that many lawyers would rather clients did not realize.

All sorts of hybrid arrangements are possible, and, as in any other business matter, a bit of ingenuity and some skill in negotiating can open up favourable horizons.

On occasion, for example, I have persuaded lawyers to *share* in the risk of a lawsuit by accepting a *reduced* hourly rate plus a premium if the outcome is favourable.

Such creative ways of dealing with the question of fees can make a lawyer and a client more effective partners in a legal action, as it brings their respective self-interests more closely into line.

85

5. *How much is this whole business likely to cost me?*

This is a question you should always ask, even though it is virtually certain that a lawyer will bend over backwards to avoid giving you an answer.

The lawyer will say – truly – that a meaningful estimate is impossible because everything depends on what the other side does.

Will the other side be cooperative or hostile? Will the other side move briskly forward or stall? Will *they* want to handle the drafting of documents, or will they leave that responsibility to you? These and other uncertainties are real enough.

Still, a client has the right to be given *some* estimate of probable fees and expenses.

Will it be in the range of $1000 or $10,000 or $100,000?

These estimates, vague as they are, are valuable because **every prospective client should do a cost-benefit analysis – if only an informal one – before embarking on any legal action.**

My close friend Gordon Forbes, a former South African tennis champion who became most successful in the electrical business, tells an amusing story about his foray into the mystical world of trying to find out what a legal bill was going to be. It seems that Gordon had a problem requiring the services of a good British law firm, but he was most concerned about what the limits of his costs might be, and queried in a persistent and pointed manner the eminent solicitor handling the case.

The response he got was: 'Well, you know, Mr Forbes, it is a bit like a piece of string, and it's really hard to tell.' Upon further persistent questioning, the response became: 'I suppose you could be looking at £20,000 to £25,000.'

Since Gordon had figured that in South Africa the services in question couldn't cost more than £2000 or so, he said to the rather shocked British attorney: 'What I would like you to do is £2000 worth of work and stop at precisely that moment, even if you are in the middle of a sentence.' The stunned recipient of those orders was so taken aback by this approach that, if you can believe it, Mr Forbes got all his legal work done within the £2000 limit.

There are no hard-and-fast rules as to what is an acceptable ratio between legal fees and total monies on the table. This ratio, in fact, varies quite widely in accordance with different procedures.

Some years ago, when IMG was in the steepest part of its growth curve – that stage when a business's very success can make it go broke – I decided to beef up our resources and facilities with the help of a quite substantial bank loan. Because of the amount of money involved and the other demands on my own time, I hired counsel to negotiate the transaction.

How much sense did it make to pay for that sort of service? Since the legal fees became, in effect, part of what I would be paying for the use of the loan, I reasoned that costs had to be kept within a point or two of the total transaction.

At the other end of the spectrum, if you are unlucky enough to find yourself the defendant in a liability suit, you may conclude that anything short of 100 per cent of the award being sought is worth giving to your attorneys; you'll grudge every penny, and rightly so, but what's the alternative?

The worst thing that ever happened to IMG in a court of law was when we spent $200,000 in legal fees en route to a settlement that cost us $800,000. That settlement, however, was in lieu of a judgment against us of $1,036,760. So, everything being relative, you could say our legal fees were well spent!

6. *Will you accept a cap on fees?*
Over the years, I have sometimes used a stratagem which has, I believe, saved our company money. But even more important, it has allowed us peace of mind and the feeling that we were staying in control of our own destiny.

In instances where legal actions threatened to become complicated and protracted, I have tried to persuade our hired counsel to agree to a *cap* on yearly fees.

This cap, to be acceptable to the attorneys, obviously has to be somewhat in excess of the estimated cost; it is meant not as a way of cutting corners, but as protection against a worst-case scenario where outlays really run away with you.

In one instance, our lawyers estimated that a certain matter would cost between $48,000 and $72,000 a year to pursue, and I suggested putting a cap at $90,000.

Now, $90,000 is an annoying sum to have to shell out for lawyers, but it's preferable to worrying that, at the end of the year, you'll tot up the bills and they'll amount to $150,000.

Why should a lawyer agree to a cap on fees?

First, because if he or she *doesn't* agree, there's a chance you will take your business to someone who will.

Second, because if he refuses, he'll be placed in the embarrassing position of having to acknowledge that he doesn't place much faith in his own estimates.

And a lawyer wouldn't want to admit that, any more than a car mechanic would. If the estimates can't be relied on, who knows what *other* aspects of the lawyer's services might turn out to be dubious.

The One-time-only Relationship

Most individuals hire lawyers on an *ad hoc* basis.

They are buying a piece of property. They are getting a divorce. They have been involved in a fender-bender and are entertaining visions of a big 'pain-and-suffering' award.

In cases like these, lawyer-client relationships tend to be short-term, with repeat business expected by no one and loyalty accruing to neither side.

Why, then, should attorneys work hard at doing a good and timely job for one-time-only customers?

Except where a contingent fee is involved, the lawyer's only incentives are his or her own professionalism and personal pride, and the client has no choice but to put a considerable amount of faith in those things.

That faith, however, should not be blind or passive.

Clients should monitor their lawyer's work *as it is being done*.

They should question fees and expenses *as the bills come in*.

If an action doesn't appear to be going well, they should demand to know why, *before it's too late for a shift in course, or, for that matter, a change in representation.*

Loyalty and Leverage

The dynamic is rather different when a lawyer-client relationship has some history behind it and, presumably, some future ahead of it.

In that case, loyalty and good business sense neatly dovetail with fear to keep lawyers on their toes and give them plenty of reasons for performing well and charging fairly.

Obviously, no attorney wants to jeopardize a long-term relationship by doing a single piece of shoddy work or by some pettiness on the billing side.

Additionally, since a lawyer and a longstanding client will almost certainly have a network of colleagues and associates in common, no attorney will want to risk a damaged reputation by negative word of mouth.

All these factors give a client leverage – leverage he should never forget that he has, but which, in a good relationship, never need be used.

When Should You Marry Your Lawyer?

In forging an ongoing relationship with an attorney, however, there are a couple of questions a client should ask himself:

Do I really *need* this relationship?

When and on what basis should I pick *my* attorney?

On the first question, I can only say that common sense must dictate the need. Some people retain lawyers month after idle month simply because it makes them feel important to have a lawyer.

On the other hand, an individual with assets substantial enough to be considered an estate will obviously want a trusted attorney he can talk to through the years. Similarly, anyone responsible for running a business will want to have access to legal counsel from someone familiar enough with the operation so that every conversation doesn't have to start from square one.

Beyond a certain size, businesses seem automatically to spawn a need for in-house counsel, and then, by the curious and distressing mechanism that makes lawyers multiply, in-house counsel always seems to come up with various needs for *outside* counsel.

As to *how* to enter into a marriage with a lawyer, I say do it gradually and with enormous circumspection.

Breaking up with one's attorney is emotionally stressful and logistically daunting, and the more miles you have travelled together, the more wrenching the whole process is. So take it slow until you're sure of the attorney's competence and of your mutual compatibility.

I am a firm believer in letting a lawyer know, early on, that if he performs well, charges fairly, and is responsive to my needs, I will have plenty more work for him in the future.

This is an absolutely basic way of providing an incentive, and of course businesses use it all the time with regard to advertising agencies, public relations firms, and so forth.

Any professional in a service occcupation will work harder if he knows that one well-done job can lead the way to a motherlode of ongoing assignments. Lawyers are no exception.

They may *act* independent. But a smart client should see beyond the professional pose and realize that, diploma or no diploma, a lawyer is a vendor who is in deep trouble unless he can hold on to your business.

PART II

---

*Lawyers and Businessmen:
the Uneasy Alliance*

5

Why Lawyers Drive Businessmen Crazy

A number of years ago, a book was published called *The Duke of Deception*. It was written by a fellow named Geoffrey Wolff, and it was about Wolff's late father, a fascinating raconteur, con man and liar. Wolff Senior was a compelling rogue who had unfailing insights into what made people tick, and who used those insights to raise petty fraud to an art form.

The Duke had a credit rating somewhat worse than the government of Mexico's, yet he managed to buy anything he wanted on credit.

He could walk into the finest men's store, and walk out again with half a dozen suits charged to a newly opened house account on which payment would never be made. He would drive convertibles away from used-car lots on the strength of a spurious promise. He'd 'buy' watches, jewellery, television sets, and he would use a variety of spiels that ranged from the ingenious to the bizarre.

He got away with it again and again. Why?

He got away with it because he had the genius to penetrate to the deepest truth about how salespeople function. *Salespeople, he realized, are so obsessed with selling that they barely notice anything else.*

In the face of an opportunity for a sale – especially a *big* sale, to an apparently wealthy customer full of swagger and the implied promise of repeat business – other considerations fade into insignificance.

Judgement grows fuzzy. If something doesn't seem exactly kosher, chances are a salesperson will overlook it. Procedures can somehow or other be bypassed if need be.

Priority number one is not to let that customer out of the door without some merchandise. The Duke understood perfectly the psychological make-up that correlates with the sales mentality, and exploited it.

To put it another way, he realized that *there are personality types that correspond with different occupations.*

This, in turn, has to do with two factors:

1. What sort of person picks what sort of career to begin with.
2. How people are affected by the pressures and traditions that pertain in various fields.

These observations go a long way towards explaining why businessmen and lawyers drive each other crazy.

Businessmen are like dogs; they're high-spirited, frisky; their tails wag at the thought of a deal.

Lawyers are like cats – careful, coy and retreating.

Put the two in a conference room together, and anything can happen.

What-if-ing a Deal to Death

The best and worst thing about lawyers, from the businessman's point of view, is that they are thorough.

Often it's good that they are, because businessmen, like salesmen, sometimes risk letting their enthusiasm for doing a deal cloud their assessment of the potential downside.

Still, there are times when lawyerly thoroughness just isn't appropriate – when the real danger is that the attorneys will get together and what-if a deal to death.

Class Will Out

Several years ago I negotiated a contract between Michael Parkinson, the British television personality, and Rupert Murdoch involving a TV series to be broadcast in Australia. The major points of the deal had all been discussed and agreed to – we knew how much Parkinson would be compensated, who would actually own the programme, how foreign rights would be divvied up, and so forth.

Appended to these crucial matters was a simple provision that Parkinson's expenses to, from, and within Australia would be paid for.

Well, this made the lawyers on both sides very nervous.

Would Parkinson be content with a single room in a hotel, or would he expect a large house with a staff, chauffeur and cars for himself and his family? Shouldn't everything be spelled out? Shouldn't a floor and a ceiling be placed on the expense budget? What if he stayed longer than expected? What if he went shopping?

What if, what if, what if?

Had all these what-ifs been addressed in the kind of detail the lawyers felt necessary, deadlines would have been missed, enthusiasm would have dissipated, and there would have been a real risk of losing the contract altogether.

Lawyers like things to be as explicit and as airtight as they can ever be. Both their personality and their training point them towards fastidiousness; and of course they live in terror of the day when something goes wrong, and a client turns on them and says: 'You idiot! Why didn't you tell me that could happen?'

But it is my contention that, in many if not most contracts, **there are certain things which, by their very nature, have to be left and should be left to trust, goodwill and common sense.**

Murdoch's lawyers had to realize – as Murdoch himself understood, of course – that Parkinson was a professional doing a job, not a freeloader off on a joyride.

And Parkinson's people had to trust that Murdoch would not simply be Parkinson's employer in Australia, but his *host*, and would therefore be nothing but generous and gracious.

To put it simply, *each side had to trust that the other had some class.*

Eventually, despite the typical 'OK, but don't blame me'

objections of the lawyers, the contract was signed with the 'fuzzy' language still intact.

Needless to say, it didn't turn out to be a problem for anyone concerned. In fact, it provided an opportunity for reaffirming the goodwill and mutual regard between our company and Mr Murdoch.

Eight months after the deal was done, at a time when the precise discussions were not very fresh in anybody's mind, Murdoch simply made good on Parkinson's expenses.

No one, with the possible exception of the lawyers, was surprised at this civilized and gentlemanly conclusion of the business.

The End Run Around the Legal Beagle

It is an absolutely basic rule of conducting business effectively that to get a favourable result, **you've got to get to the decision maker.**

Of all the many ways that time, effort and money are wasted in business, probably one of the worst is talking to people who can't really help you even if they wanted to.

Getting to the decision maker is not always easy, of course; in fact, I would argue that the true meaning of the word 'clout' is *access*.

There are any number of obstacles that can interfere with access – and lawyers happen to be one of them. **One of the main things that drive businessmen crazy about lawyers is that lawyers will generally do everything to prevent you from talking directly to their clients.**

There are several reasons for this, and some are more praiseworthy than others.

Lawyers would like you to *think* they are keeping you away from the principal because they have a sacred obligation to do so; they have been hired to protect the client from complications and annoyances, and to advance his interests without causing him any bother.

And of course there are some clients who instruct their attorneys to do exactly that.

At the risk of sounding cynical, however, I would have to say that, in my experience, when lawyers keep you away from their client, *it has at least as much to do with their own desires and convenience as with their role of protectors.*

As long as the lawyers know more of what is going on than do the actual players, they are in control. They control the pace of the proceedings – which is to say, they have a large role in determining how much will be rung up in hourly fees.

They control the *tone* of the proceedings – whether the atmosphere will be friendly and cooperative, or will take on the hostile overtones that waste time and erode goodwill.

Unless a businessman is content to leave his fate in the hands of the attorneys, then there are times when he has to end-run around them, protocol be damned.

First, Know Who the Decision Maker Is

Complicating matters is the fact that, even without stonewalling by attorneys, tracking down the decision maker can be a bedevilling process. It's such a crucial aspect of doing business, however, that I think it's worthy of a brief digression.

I still remember when, back in the early days of IMG, the person I most wanted to meet in the entire world was the chairman of the board of General Motors International. Here was the man who headed up the biggest company on earth, who controlled resources which, for all practical purposes, were infinite; here, in a word, was the man who could afford to buy absolutely everything I was so intent on selling.

Well, to make a long story short, I worked for *two years* to get a meeting with the chairman. I angled for introductions; I cashed in favours owed to me.

When I finally got my meeting, he greeted me with a fraternal handclasp and motioned me into an enormous leather chair. 'What can I do for you, Mark?' he asked, and I felt as if I had died and gone to heaven.

It took me about two minutes to realize he could do *zero* for me, and that my grand ideas about having him as an ally had been a fantasy.

In fact, the chairman operated solely in a staff capacity. His job, essentially, was to pass along corporate policies to the various GM subsidiaries, whose general managers were almost autonomous when it came to decisions of interest to IMG.

The time I spent trying to get that meeting was not altogether wasted, however. I learned a valuable lesson from it: **take nothing for granted about where the decision-making authority actually lies. Look for the subtleties. Assume nothing.**

And understand that every organization is different.

Consider Rolex. For many years, IMG has had a terrific relationship with Rolex, whose brilliant chairman and managing director, André Heiniger, is a businessman for whom I have the very highest regard.

Heiniger, like any good executive, is consistent – but consistent *in his own way*. He leaves most marketing decisions to his local representatives and managers around the world; *however*, on issues that are clearly multinational in scope, he insists on personally handing down the final word from Geneva.

The challenge is figuring out where, with a global firm like Rolex, you draw the line between what's 'multinational' and what isn't. You have to try to think along with the person on the other side – and thinking along with Heiniger is a strenuous but worthwhile exercise!

These intuitions get trickier the farther afield you go, culturally speaking – as I learned some years ago at a tiny conference table in Japan.

At this point in time, any Western businessman with any sophistication at all is aware that to do business successfully with the Japanese, it's helpful to lay aside one's usual assumptions, biases, and habits of mind. Still, in the heat of selling or negotiating – and under the influence of trans-Pacific jet lag – that is not so easily accomplished.

I had flown to Tokyo, at the request of Toyota, to discuss Toyota's possible sponsorship of the women's professional tennis circuit. An executive from our Tokyo office joined me, and we were escorted to a cramped and totally unadorned conference room with a puny table and four simple chairs.

In walked a Japanese gentleman named Soe, who handed me a card that read 'Assistant Manager'.

I saw that title and a wave of unpleasant emotions swept through me. First of all, though I make it a policy to leave my ego at the door when embarking on any negotiation, it was difficult not to feel insulted having travelled fifteen hours only to meet someone from the lower-middle management.

More to the point, I couldn't imagine that this fellow could possibly have the authority to say yea or nay on the multimillion-dollar package I had come to discuss. But I put on a brave face, and made my pitch.

To my great surprise, within a few weeks IMG got a telex from Toyota, confirming that it had decided to sponsor women's tennis on a worldwide basis.

The 'assistant manager', Japanese style, had in fact had discretion far in excess of anything an American would have expected.

As a bit of practical advice, I would urge you to be sensitive to the Mr Soes of this world, who wield their clout quietly without the armour of a fancy title. Sometimes they can do more for you than the chairman of the board!

Showdown at Pebble Beach

But again, when lawyers are screening out the person in charge, there are times when they have to be gone around or bulldozed.

Back in the 1960s, in the early days of our company, I had an object lesson in this which still strikes me as valuable.

In those years, IMG's main involvement was with golf, and we were fortunate in having as clients both Arnold Palmer and Gary Player. Aside from being superlative athletes, Arnold and Gary were highly poised, attractive and utterly professional; they were constantly in demand and it was a great pleasure to handle their business.

At some point we were asked to arrange a deal between

the Lincoln-Mercury division of the Ford Motor Company, as sponsors, and the Revue Studios subsidiary of MCA, as producers, to do a series of shows called *Challenge Golf*, in which Palmer and Player would compete against other two-man teams.

The negotiations were entirely amiable, and a contract was soon signed which provided, among other things, that the matches would be filmed during a ninety-day period at various golf courses within the state of California. In the course of the discussions, some specific venues had been talked about, but in the spirit of reason and cooperation that then prevailed, there seemed no need to spell them out in the written agreement.

The plot thickened, however, when the bean counters from Revue sat down with their adding machines and figured out that the studio could save a fair amount of money by filming all the matches on courses in and around Los Angeles. There would be less overtime to pay, and no travel and lodging expenses for crews and production executives.

So Revue's lawyers scoured the contract, and – what do you know? – there was nothing in it that said the matches *couldn't* all be played right there in Los Angeles and Orange counties!

There was only one small problem with this plan: Lincoln-Mercury's general manager, Chase Morsey, remembered quite specifically that during the negotiations it had been clearly understood that some of the matches would take place in northern California, and that one, in particular, would be played at Pebble Beach – a glamorous and upscale club with which Lincoln-Mercury wanted, understandably, to be associated.

Now Morsey got *his* lawyers on to the case, trying to find something in the contract that gave Lincoln-Mercury the right of approval on the choice of courses, or, if need be, to tank the agreement together.

By this point everyone was getting mad at everyone, and a deal that had begun as a love feast was giving everybody headaches.

As it turned out, however, the stalemate was easily broken by a single phone call from Morsey to Lew Wasserman, the chairman of MCA.

Morsey told Wasserman his side of the story, and Wasserman, in turn, confronted his people with a single question: 'Did you or did you not lead the executives of Lincoln-Mercury to believe there would be a show produced at Pebble Beach?'

He didn't want to know what the contract said.

He didn't want to know about his company's legal rights.

He didn't want to hear about what the change in venue would cost.

He just wanted an answer to that simple question.

When MCA's people acknowledged that there *had* been talk about a match at Pebble Beach, Wasserman told them to apologize to Morsey, dispatch a crew to Carmel pronto, and stop wasting everybody's time.

In that single exchange, Morsey and Wasserman not only got *Challenge Golf* back on track, but cemented the relationship between their two companies by making it clear that each would stand by its commitments, whether or not those commitments were expressed in letter-perfect legal form.

Telephone

Two factors enabled Morsey and Wasserman to resolve their problem so efficiently: good faith and good communication.

Both are essential for mutually advantageous business dealings. **Both are often mucked up by lawyers.**

Remember Chinese whispers, and everybody laughing at how much the original message had changed?

Well, going back and forth between lawyers who won't let their clients speak directly is a lot like that – but with two significant differences.

One difference is that it's hard to laugh when the garbling of the message is costing you cash, credibility, and maybe a relationship.

The second difference is that the garbling doesn't come

about by simple mumbling, but by *a clash of differing styles and agendas.*

Let me give you an example of how this game of poor communication works in practice.

A few years ago, IMG negotiated a deal with Sony, whereby Sony would sponsor the world computerized ranking system of men's professional golf. Among the provisions of the deal was a perfectly clear understanding that Sony and IMG would work together to stage *three simultaneous press conferences – in New York, London and Tokyo – to launch the new arrangement.*

Then the deal, as drafted by executives, went to the attorneys.

Here's what happened to the press-conference provision once the lawyers got hold of it:

First it got garbled so that three *separate* events were staged in the cities mentioned above, so the impact of simultaneity was lost.

Then it was misinterpreted to mean that Sony and IMG had an ongoing responsibility to hold press conferences together – a responsibility that *neither* side particularly wanted.

Then it became mangled to the point where it was thought that IMG and Sony were supposed to hold a press conference before *every* event on the pro tour!

I would never even have *known* about this last distortion, except that I got a call one day from our New York office informing me that the Sony people were very upset with us.

'Upset about what?' I asked.

'Upset that the press conference in Chicago was a flop.'

'*What* press conference in Chicago?'

And so it went, until we struggled our way back through the morass of legalese and finally uncovered the original message.

Not By Law Alone

Just as sound business judgement dictates that there are instances when the best move is to go around the lawyers, there are also situations when the wisest action is to go around the law itself.

By this I certainly don't mean that it's acceptable to *break* the law. It's only that, **in certain situations, an issue that seems legal at first glance is in fact more effectively approached in pragmatic and nontechnical business terms.**

Selling the Cup

The truth of this notion was demonstrated recently by a controversy involving the Royal Perth Yacht Club, which we represent.

When the Australian sailors defeated the Americans at Newport, Rhode Island, in 1983, the ownership of the famous America's Cup moved to Perth. For the New York Yacht Club, the loss was more than just a psychological blow: the licensing of the America's Cup name and logo is quite a considerable revenue source that goes a long way towards underwriting the races and, in fact, towards keeping the entire sport of competitive yachting afloat.

The New Yorkers, for whom lack of confidence has never been a problem, had apparently never given a thought to what would happen to their cash flow if they ever lost the Cup, apparently because it never dawned on them that they might be beaten.

Having lost the trophy, however, and in keeping with their habit of changing the rules when the game was no longer going their way, the New York Yacht Club began refusing to assign trademark applications around the world for the exclusive licensing rights to the name and the logo of the America's Cup.

At first glance, what was developing seemed to be a legal battle, and a fascinating one at that. In some jurisdictions, ownership of a trademark is determined by first use, irrespective of first filing; in other places, rights go to the first filer, regardless of who was the first user. Then there was the intriguing question of whether licensing rights automatically went with the ownership of the Cup itself or were to be regarded as a separate entity. The issues were complex and juicy enough to keep several batteries of copyright and trademark lawyers busy for many months, if not for several years.

In the meantime, however, the Royal Perth Yacht Club had a multimillion-dollar event to stage, and, because of the New York Yacht Club's filings around the world, Perth was running into obstacle after obstacle in arranging the fees and royalties to which, by common sense and simple justice, it was entitled as host club of the races.

With time before the 1987 Cup defence growing ever shorter, it became clear that in regarding the trademark business as a legal squabble, Perth was agreeing to fight the battle on New York's chosen turf, and by doing so was effectively conceding defeat. *Time was the real enemy, as it so often is when litigation looms.*

The solution – simple enough once we thought of it – was to stop arguing in legal terms and shift the battle back to business basics.

Accordingly, at a meeting in Australia late in 1985, I suggested to the officers of the Royal Perth that they call off their attorneys and instead write a simple letter to the New York Yacht Club as well as to all other competing parties.

The letter should say essentially this: If anyone did anything to hamper the Royal Perth Yacht Club's efforts to market the 1987 defence *in exactly the same way that it had been marketed in years past by the New York Yacht Club*, that party would be barred from racing at Perth. Period.

Would such a prohibition be legal? My contention was that it would be; it would certainly be just.

But I knew that the threat of disqualification would never be put to the test because now it would be the *other* side racing against time and taking on the risk.

Would the New York Yacht Club, having spent millions on new equipment, jeopardize its chances of being allowed on the starting line Down Under – especially knowing that if it challenged the validity of the Royal Perth edict, the matter would have to be tried in the jurisdiction of Western Australia?

So, strictly speaking, the trademark issue was never solved;

it was simply made to disappear. Perhaps such a resolution might be disappointing to a legal scholar. For a businessman, it was the most expedient and least costly of all possible outcomes.

The Force of Shame

A great deal has been written about the real or perceived decline of business ethics, and about the shameless shenanigans of certain highly visible businessmen.

However, I would argue that, as a group, business people are as concerned as ever with their good names – and *appeals to their sense of shame can sometimes be a highly effective way of avoiding litigation and finding short cuts around legal dilemmas.*

Let me illustrate this by way of an anecdote, though it may be significant that the company involved was Japanese, and perhaps more prone to compunction than its American counterparts.

In 1986 Harvard University celebrated its 350th anniversary, and the Harvard Corporation hired IMG to handle the licensing of products and promotions connected with the event.

Accordingly, we did a worldwide survey of how 'Harvard' this and 'Harvard' that were being marketed. We discovered that there was a company in Japan – where the name is hugely prestigious – calling *itself* 'Harvard'. This company had been doing about $10 million worth of business a year for the past decade, and had never paid the university a dime in royalties!

At first glance, this seemed like the most flagrant sort of piracy, though there was more to it than met the eye.

Back in the mid-1970s, executives of this Japanese firm had in fact visited Cambridge, Mass., with the intention of working out a licensing arrangement with the Harvard Corporation. Prior to the 350th anniversary, however, Harvard hadn't wanted to sully itself with the taint of commerce, and its officials wouldn't even talk to the Japanese businessmen.

Piqued by this rebuff, the Japanese went back to Tokyo, where they discovered that the name 'Harvard' had never been filed as a trademark *within Japan*. They registered it and had been operating in accord with Japanese law ever since.

So, we once again faced an intriguing legal situation – one that might have kept a pack of attorneys profitably employed for a long time.

Our counsel in Tokyo, however, pulled a *business* masterpiece that cut a terrific path through the potential legal morass.

He called a meeting and patiently listened while the other side's lawyers aggressively spelled out all the reasons why the company was right. It had *tried* to do business with the university, and been turned away. It had complied with all appropriate local statutes. It had invested time and money, and taken significant risks to make this a successful enterprise – *now* the university was hitting it up for a percentage?

Our counsel heard the lawyers out, and realized that they were trying a little too hard to protest their innocence; there was an undertone of guilty conscience.

So our lawyer calmly announced that he understood their position and wouldn't fight them after all. To clarify matters, however, *he would send a memo to everyone the company did business with, explaining why it didn't see fit to pay a royalty for the use of the Harvard name!*

The licensing arrangement was summarily concluded.

Ac-cen-tuate the Positive, E-lim-inate the Negative

In 1968 I negotiated a contract with John DeLorean, then the general manager of the Pontiac division of General Motors. The contract involved Pontiac's sponsorship of the US Ski Team and the US Ski Association, and there was a high level of enthusiasm for the arrangement in all quarters.

At a meeting in which DeLorean and I discussed the major deal points, and at which Pontiac's attorneys were present, John turned to his lawyers, waved his finger at them in mock scolding, and said, 'I really want this thing, and don't you guys screw it up.'

This vignette graphically summarizes another important axiom:

> ### McCormack's Axiom of Checks and Balances
> Businessmen accentuate the positive, lawyers are left to wrestle with the negative, and all parties struggle towards a situation somewhere in between.

Since this meeting took place at General Motors, let me put it in these terms. The businessman – the one who wants the deal – is the gas pedal; he provides the forward momentum, the thrust, the push that gets things started.

The lawyer is the brake; his job is to keep things within a safe speed and to stop the machine at any sign of trouble.

When the brake and the gas pedal are in balance, the vehicle of business runs smoothly.

The point I would like to make, however, is this: until the car is rolling, a brake pedal is redundant. And if the brake is applied from the beginning, chances are the momentum will never get a chance to build.

For that reason, **I am a firm believer in keeping the lawyers out of the early stages of a deal.**

Why contemplate the things that can go wrong before savouring the things that can go right?

Why create the anxiety that inevitably attaches to the presence of lawyers before establishing the enthusiasm that attends the care and feeding of a deal?

Eventually, of course, lawyers do need to get involved, and I freely admit that there is a potential downside to bringing them into a deal late.

Sometimes, inevitably, effort must be duplicated.

Sometimes, for technical reasons, certain deal points need revising.

And then there's the discomfort of dealing with lawyers who are testy about not having been consulted sooner.

But I contend that in the great majority of cases, **business ends are better served by stressing the positive up front and**

dealing with the negative only after the momentum is established and agreement in principle has been achieved.

Why Businessmen Drive Lawyers Crazy

But let's be fair.

If lawyers sometimes drive businessmen to fits of rage and
distraction, the terrible truth is that the opposite is also true.

If businessmen, in the throes of frustration, sometimes view
lawyers as obstructionist killjoys who gum up the works and
prevent people from making a living, then it's also true that
attorneys, at moments of crisis, think of deal makers as
irresponsible cowboys who would all end up bankrupt, or
worse, were it not for the intervention of cooler heads.

In this connection, I must relate the sad saga of a man
named Chuck Sullivan. Sullivan is a scion of the family that
owns the New England Patriots and is himself the owner of
Sullivan Stadium, in which the team plays. He is a highly
educated and sophisticated man – and he even has a law
degree! In his heart, however, he is a businessman, with all
the enthusiasms and occasional excesses pertaining thereto.

A few years ago, Sullivan decided that he was going to
make himself a ton of money by aligning himself with pop
singer Michael Jackson. At the time, Jackson was the hottest
property since the Beatles, and it seemed that *anything* –
clothing, fragrances, soft drinks – could be marketed in his
name. Accordingly, Sulllivan reputedly shelled out around
$50 million as promoter of the Jackson family's 1984 concert
tour, and committed an additional $30 million for the licen-
sing rights to Jackson's name and likeness.

In fantasy, Sullivan had pulled off a real coup. In reality,
he had locked himself into a disaster.

The concert tour entailed such enormous transportation,
staging and insurance costs that in spite of sellouts every-
where, it reportedly lost more than a million dollars.

When the tour was over, Jackson's managers became fearful
that he was being 'overexposed'. This meant that, just when

Sullivan was trying to sublicense Jackson's name, no one was hearing as much about Jackson anymore!

Having already incurred losses, Sullivan approached IMG for help in disposing of the licensing rights he controlled. He showed us his contracts, and our attorneys were frankly surprised that a man of Sullivan's sophistication could have got himself into unworkable contract provisions.

Sullivan's story perfectly illustrates several classic mistakes made by overfervent deal makers, and points up exactly what businessmen *should* look to lawyers for:

1. He very probably saw dollar signs that were unrealistically large. Whatever the potential windfall, $80 million was too big an exposure to risk in a business as volatile as pop music.

2. He was possibly too intent on being where the action was. It might make great cocktail-party conversation to be able to describe oneself as Michael Jackson's impresario, but level-headed advice would have pointed out the downside.

3. He was perhaps too single-mindedly intent on sealing the deal, and Jackson's lawyers, sensing that Sullivan would agree to almost anything to get the contract, again and again put him on the short end of clauses that unemotional outside advice would not have allowed him to accept.

The Deal Memo to the Rescue

Given, then, that lawyers can bust up a deal if brought in too soon, and that businessmen can get themselves into no end of trouble if lawyers are brought in too late, how can deal makers and their attorneys stay usefully in sync?

One way is by effective use of the *deal memo*.

The deal memo is an integral part of how we do business at IMG. Here's how it works.

One of our executives negotiates the points of a deal – *but* it is made clear to all concerned that he or she does not have the authority to *conclude* that deal.

The executive then writes a deal memo – just a letter, in plain English – to the legal department, outlining the agreement that's been negotiated. This deal memo serves several purposes:

1. Since it will involve the legal department *before* any commitment has been made, it justifies keeping the lawyers out of the early talks.

2. It forces the executive to be *crystal clear* about what has or hasn't been agreed to, since it has to be put in writing.

3. It allows the executive and the lawyers to work together, away from the pressures of the negotiating table, to put the final document in optimal form.

4. When necessary, it provides a mechanism to let us stall for time or simply pause for breath.

Theory versus Practice

The theory of the deal memo is simplicity itself, and at our company it is regarded as an absolutely standard procedure.

Yet, at one time or another, virtually everyone who negotiates for IMG has given in to businessman's impulsiveness and neglected to do a proper memo.

This drives our legal department batty – and rightly so.

The lawyers' annoyance is not to do with mere protection of their bailiwick, but with substantive issues.

If a deal memo isn't done, or is done improperly, and if the eventual contract doesn't accurately reflect the deal maker's understanding of the terms, whose fault is it?

Worse still, if an account executive skirts the legal department, and unilaterally sends his customer a writing that could be *construed* as constituting a contract, could IMG be held to that agreement?

To avoid this latter possibility, our general counsel, Bill Carpenter, is *constantly* coaching us on exculpatory language that *every* business negotiator should have as part of his or her working vocabulary:

'If this reflects our understanding, I will have the
contracts drawn up,' or
'If this is correct, I will arrange to have it finalized.'

Phrases like these can save an enormous amount of trouble,
and will steer you clear of being held to commitments you
didn't even *know* you'd made.

Down, Boy!

Before leaving the subject of how lawyers can sometimes save
over-eager executives from themselves, let me give one more
brief example of this dynamic in action.

At IMG, as agents we are hardly ever in a position to
commit our clients to anything: we *advise* our clients; our
clients commit themselves.

This is an extraordinarily basic distinction, designed for the
protection of all parties; you don't need a law degree or an
MBA to grasp either the notion itself or the reasoning behind
it.

Still, in the midst of deal lust, it's truly amazing how often
even this rudimentary point is overlooked.

Not long ago, one of our junior line executives was approached regarding a lucrative clothing endorsement for a
client. Over the course of several long conversations, during
which a lot of intoxicating numbers were bandied about, our
young executive's ardour grew to the point where he made
the endorsement sound like a done deal – regardless of the
facts that:

1. The final authority to conclude the agreement rested
not with him but with the client.
2. The proposed endorsement, unbeknown to the
eager young executive, was in clear conflict with an
agreement signed before he had come on board.

The legal department (by way of a deal memo!) caught the
potential problem, and the upshot was nothing worse than
some wasted time and some deserved embarrassment on the
would-be deal maker's part. Had Legal not been on the case,

111

well, all of us could have had a real problem on our hands.

The point is that while there *are* broad differences in style and priorities among businessmen and lawyers, and while those differences inevitably give rise to tension, *that tension can be a blessing as well as a bane*.

If businessmen and lawyers are natural adversaries, they are natural allies, too.

They temper each other's excesses and compensate for each other's deficiencies. And when they work effectively together, they can achieve results beyond what either group could accomplish alone.

6

Playing as a Team

Can't Live with 'Em; Can't Live without 'Em;

So goes the old saying about relations between men and women.

The maxim could apply equally to the difficult but necessary marriage between business people and attorneys.

Yes, the two groups get on each other's nerves almost every hour of every working day.

Yes, members of each profession are only too ready to point out the foibles and pretensions of the other.

Still, lawyers and business types are unmistakably symbiotic. Without business clients, a hefty proportion of attorneys would have absolutely nothing to do. And without lawyers . . . well, I happen to believe that businessmen could get on all right without attorneys, as long as *none* of them had attorneys.

But that's too much to hope for in this life.

You can bet that the fellow across the conference table from you is going to have a legal eagle or two on his side. That being so, you had better have counsel on your team, too.

And you had better make sure that the machinery that connects your lawyer and yourself is running smoothly because, as I've stated below:

McCormack's Axiom of Symbiosis

The successful outcome of a negotiation or a legal fight most often depends not just on the individual savvy of the business person and the lawyer involved, but on how well they function *together*.

113

Of all the many ways in which business people interact with their own attorneys, probably the most usual, *but also one of the most crucial*, has to do with the drawing up of contracts.

Turning a verbal understanding into a written agreement should be a dynamic and creative process. It shouldn't just lock in a deal, but enhance it.

Unfortunately, the terrible truth is that contracts are too often drawn up without any creativity at all, and I shudder to think about the opportunities that are lost that way.

Why are those opportunities wasted?

Because of bad communication between the deal makers and the attorneys, or because of arrogance on one or both sides.

In the worst case, the line person who made the deal is pigheaded enough to imagine that he or she has thought of everything, that the deal points that have been negotiated could not possibly be improved upon, and that the lawyer's job consists of nothing more than the passive translation of the deal memo into legalese.

This attitude is in clear violation of the following:

McCormack's Axiom of Inevitable Omissions

No one *ever* thinks of everything.

This kind of deal maker seldom takes the time actually to *talk* to the lawyers – why bother, if the lawyers are expected to have no substantive input?

A similar boondoggle results if it's the *attorneys* who over-play their own particular role at the expense of fruitful team-work.

Some lawyers, overly proud of their own areas of expertise, take it upon themselves to make substantive changes in aspects of deals that they are not really in a position to understand. This type of lawyer likes to knock off the rough edges, so that the finished contract is a marvel of symmetry and elegance –

regardless of the fact that sometimes it's the rough edges in which a deal's real benefits appear!

A Shakespearean Masterpiece

If jealousy, parochialism, and lack of communication can lead to contracts that are less advantageous than they ought to be, then good communication and a mutual regard for each other's skills and resources can bring about the optimal functioning of the businessman–lawyer combination.

Let me illustrate this optimal functioning by way of an example.

In 1965 we were approached, on behalf of our client Gary Player, by the Shakespeare Company. Shakespeare, for many years a leader in the manufacture of fishing rods, had decided to get into the golf business with a line of fibreglass clubs.

They wanted an endorsement from Player and in exchange were offering him royalites on all fibreglass clubs sold under the Shakespeare name, as well as on all fibreglass shafts sold by Shakespeare to other manufacturers. The royalties were to be applied against very substantial guarantees, and by the standards of 1965, the whole package constituted a huge commitment to Gary. Shakespeare's management was very high on the new golf venture, and negotiations were proceeding with great enthusiasm and goodwill.

Still, there are certain technicalities that must be dealt with in every contract. For one thing, terms must be precisely, *legally* defined. But how exactly does one define a golf club?

Our lawyers defined it as 'a shaft connected to a head with a hossel'. As it turned out, that careful and painstaking definition benefited our client by some thousands of dollars – and also gave us an opportunity to cement our relationship with Shakespeare.

Shortly after the Shakespeare deal was completed, Player was approached by the Lampkin Leather Grip Company, which wanted him to endorse its grips on *whatever* clubs he used.

Now, we knew that Shakespeare had no plans to get into

the golf-grip business, so there was no conflict on that score. We also knew that it was established practice for pro golfers to endorse grips separately from clubs.

Still, the deal with Shakespeare was quite unusual by its sheer size, and we felt we owed the company a degree of loyalty. So we went to the company executives and told them about the Lampkin offer. We pointed out that our contract – because *it made no mention of grips* in its definition of a golf club – *did* give us the legal right to enter into a separate grips endorsement; we assured them, however, that we wouldn't take the Lampkin offer if Shakespeare felt it was a violation of the *spirit* of our agreement.

Putting it that way, of course, brought human nature into the equation. The executives of the Shakespeare Company appreciated both being consulted and our willingness *not* to take selfish advantage of technicalities in the contract. In the end, they graciously gave us permission to enter into the Lampkin deal.

Far from breeding ill will – which might have resulted if the Shakespeare executives felt we were trying to 'get around' them – the incident set a tone of above-board dealing and mutual consideration.

And it all came about because the lawyers foresaw all sorts of possibilities in the original wording of the contract.

'Good Cop'/'Bad Cop'

Cooperating in the conceiving and drafting of contracts is one of *many* ways in which lawyers and executives can help each other shine.

Another way has to do with the roles they adopt in negotiations.

Consider the 'good cop'/'bad cop' scenario – one of the most brilliant and versatile negotiating tactics ever devised.

The name derives from the classic instance of two police investigators working together to get a suspect to confess. The 'bad cop' plays the heavy, the one who bullies, needles and threatens the suspect, acts utterly convinced of the suspect's guilt, and tells the hapless interviewee that he is certain to 'get the chair'.

The 'good cop', on the other hand, is all patience and compassion. He soothes, he mollifies, he acts as if he believes the suspect's story. He even tells his partner to 'lay off the poor guy'.

In the quintessential case, what happens is that the bad cop leaves the room to get a pack of cigarettes, and the suspect confesses to the good cop!

In part, the criminal has let himself believe that the fellow is really on his side. On a deeper psychological level, however, what motivates him to confess is probably that the pressure applied by the bad cop has given him an irresistible need for a sympathetic ear. In precinct-house parlance, he has been 'softened up'.

For business people and lawyers, too, the good cop/bad cop strategy can move mountains – if you know how to use it.

Few things in the world are easier than casting a lawyer in the role of villain. Let's face it – the other side is inclined to think the worst of your attorneys, and the attorneys themselves, with a kind of bulldog glee, seem to delight in being thought of as the bad guys, the street fighters, the stalwarts who won't give an inch.

The subtler part of the equation lies in how the businessman plays *his* part – how he uses the lawyers' toughness to make his own softer sell seem that much more appealing.

A few years ago, I suggested to the All-England Club that we undertake a worldwide programme to license the Wimbledon name on tennis-related products.

This, as you may imagine, was vastly complicated. Hundreds of products called 'Wimbledon' something or other were already being marketed in dozens of jurisdictions around the globe. Some companies were paying royalties and some were not. Some had registered trademarks that might or might not stand up in court, and some were going blithely along with no trademark at all.

Further complicating the issue was the fact that 'Wimbledon' is not just the name of a sports championship, in the way the US Open means just that and nothing more; it is also the name of a London borough as well as a well-known soccer club.

If the legal issues were hazy, the moral and economic ones were crystal clear: people were unfairly cashing in on the Wimbledon name, and it was costing the rightful owners of the name a lot of money.

We decided on a two-pronged strategy to remedy the situation. Our lawyers would play the bad cop, harassing the unlicensed users of the name, bringing a suit where necessary. Meanwhile, I would play the good cop. I would gently try to persuade the companies, first of all, that what they were doing simply wasn't right, and second, that they would in fact do much better if they paid a proper royalty, in exchange for which they would gain the prestige, expertise and marketing clout of the entire Wimbledon machinery.

Part of the beauty of this arrangement was that it really didn't have a downside. The All-England Club and IMG agreed from the start that at no point would more money be spent on lawyers than was brought in from fees made on licensing arrangements.

From the beginning, we understood that neither aspect of our approach was likely to succeed without the other. Without my dangling the carrot of greater revenues that would result from the full cooperation of All-England, the lawyers' stick would not have been impressive. At the very least, unlicensed users of the Wimbledon name could have stalled for several years, and in certain jurisdictions, frankly, they probably would have won the right to keep on using it.

On the other hand, without the threat presented by the lawyers, people already making money from the tournament would have been less inclined to listen to my sales pitch – why give up a piece of the pie if you don't have to?

By working together, however, the lawyers and I were able to shift the terms of the discussions. Instead of deciding *whether* they were going to bother to deal with us at all, our target companies now had a choice as to *which part of our team to deal with.*

118

Psychologically, I think the decision-making process on the part of the manufacturers came down to this. The lawyers are saying bad things about us and threatening to make trouble, and this McCormack guy seems polite and cooperative by comparison, so we may as well play ball with McCormack.

The upshot of the strategy was a welcome clarification in the rules governing use of the Wimbledon name, as well as a tremendous increase in revenues accruing to the All-England Club.

And, in fact, at least some of the manufacturers who had been using the Wimbledon name without permission actually went on to make far more money once they had come into the licensing fold.

The most dramatic instance occurred with the Nike shoe company, which had been marketing a 'Wimbledon' tennis shoe in a very lukewarm way. Once the relationship between Nike and the All-England Club was made explicit and mutual, however, promotion of the shoe became far more sophisticated and sales burgeoned.

So the story ends well for all concerned – and *it would not have happened that way unless the lawyers had been standing by snarling, subtly persuading people to deal with me instead of them.*

Ways to Skin a Cat Department

Look at almost any sort of legal contract, and what do you see?

Chances are you see a thick and inscrutable document, written in a language never spoken by the human race, and weighed down with all sorts of standardized clauses, disclaimers upon disclaimers, and riders that seem to unsay half of what has already been said.

Probably the last word that would occur to you to describe this sort of contract is 'playful'.

Yet I would arlgue that 'playful' is exactly what a well-thought-out contract ought to be – or *can* be.

I certainly don't mean playful in the sense of frivolous; any

119

businessman or lawyer who approaches contracts in that spirit won't be around for very long.

I mean playful in the sense of imaginative.

They don't teach it this way in law schools, but contracts, like negotiations, call for an ability to improvise, to implement strategies, to arrive spontaneously at a way of doing things differently than they have been done before.

You Can't Blame Me for Trying

In drafting a contract, for example, it's a playful and also useful tactic to include certain things you *know* you won't get.

Some years ago I negotiated a contract with Dunlop in Australia on behalf of one of the world's leading tennis players.

The opportunity to do this deal came about essentially because of the enthusiasm and vision of the then manager of Dunlop's tennis division Down Under. He saw the tennis boom coming sooner than most. He wanted to invest heavily in promotion, and he wanted our client.

We were so impressed with his attitude that we wrote in a clause saying that if he, at some future date, no longer ran the tennis division, our client would have the option of terminating the contract.

We were well aware, of course, that no sane legal department or upper management was likely to agree to such a provision – from their perspective, it was nothing but downside.

Still, we felt that there was a twofold psychological advantage in including it in our draft.

First of all, *it was hugely flattering* to the manager; it made him look great in the eyes of his superiors and thereby cemented his alliance with us.

Second, *it sent a message* to the others at Dunlop that we expected this person's level of commitment to be carried through by anyone we dealt with at the company.

Eventually the deal was concluded minus that playful

clause, but the thinking behind it had registered with all concerned.

Pulling the Plug

To say that a contact is playful is essentially the same as saying it is **responsive to the realities of human nature.**

Human nature is *partly* logical. It is also partly motivated by hopes and fears, vanities and insecurities, needs for reassurance and the possibility of escape.

A well-thought-out contract should address *all* the facets that make people tick.

Let me illustrate this by describing a contract provision that has proved so useful over the years that we have given it an unofficial name: the 'Australian Termination Clause'.

This clause was born during a negotiation we were handling on behalf of Jack Nicklaus with Slazenger of Australia. All the major deal points had been hashed over and agreed to – with the exception of those clauses setting forth the term of the contract, circumstances under which the agreement might be ended, and the amount of notice required for its termination.

These were sticky issues because Slazenger was gambling on a new line of products to be released under the Nicklaus name. The company was throwing a lot of money into the launch, and it was paying Jack very sizable guarantees.

If, for any reason, the new products didn't fly, Slazenger didn't want to be locked into paying the annuities on top of other losses it might possibly sustain.

Our position in the negotiation was the opposite, and equally valid. Nicklaus was one of the most marketable names in all of sport. Why should he risk sudden termination of an income-producing deal if a sales campaign flopped through no fault of his? If the Slazenger arrangement fizzled, years might go by before another similar deal offered itself in the Australian market.

How could these two positions be reconciled?

Our solution was a clause that stated that the agreement

121

could be terminated by either party at any time *but on five years' notice*.

This was acceptable to Slazenger because it put a cap on the company's liability; in exchange for the option to call it quits, Slazenger was willing to commit to five years in guarantees, during which period it would most likely have inventory to dispose of anyway.

But while the deal made sense for the manufacturer, I frankly think we got the better bargain for our client. That five-year window would have been more than enough time to find a new endorsement for Jack.

More than that, however, we felt sure that the necessity of paying off five years' worth of hefty guarantees would be a strong inducement to Slazenger not to terminate the deal. Slazenger's strategy was a defensive one; it wanted an escape hatch against worst-case possibilities – and it was willing to pay for it. But the company paid so much for that escape hatch that, in turn, it had to protect itself by making sure the Nicklaus line of products succeeded.

This, by the way, is exactly what happened. Slazenger, using its obligation to Nicklaus as a measure, put appropriate sums and energy into promoting and marketing the line, and the arrangement between the company and Jack lasted for decades.

The beauty part of the Australian Termination Clause, then, is that **by making it expensive to pull the plug, this goes a long way towards assuring that the plug won't be pulled at all.**

Letting Deals Breathe

As I said before, it is a common but costly mistake to regard a contract as a totally formal, standardized, matter-of-fact document.

In actuality, **a contract is an ongoing process, an arrangement whose nuances are constantly changing.**

Obviously, the *words* of the contract stay the same.

Nonetheless, the *implications* of those words are always evolving.

And among the crucial tasks that lawyers should perform on behalf of businessmen are:

- to fashion contracts in such a way that they can accommodate growth and change while maintaining a dynamic balance between the parties' advantages;
- to monitor and act upon the opportunities that arise once contracts are in effect and have taken on a life of their own.

A comparison to child rearing seems irresistible here. If you simply 'give birth' to a contract, then walk away, you have shirked a very major responsibility; the other part of the job lies in the care and feeding of the contract.

Milking the Penguin

Maybe the best way to illustrate the importance of creating contracts that can 'grow' is to point out what happens to those that *can't* – arrangements that are brittle, rigid, and incapable of flowing with changed circumstances.

Back in the late 1950s, when pro golf was rather an infant enterprise, and before Arnold Palmer had become a client of ours, he entered into a long-term contract with Munsingwear, the clothing manufacturer with the familiar penguin logo.

The contract called for an incredibly puny guarantee – $1000 or $2000 a year, as I recall – which was fairly standard at the time the agreement was made, but which became increasingly absurd from year to year.

Had Arnold been a client when the Munsingwear deal was offered, we would have strenuously advised him against accepting it – not necessarily because of where the contract *started*, but because there was nowhere for it to go. As it was, we spent a lot of time thinking about how best to extricate Palmer from an arrangement that had ceased to have any relation to his value on the open market.

123

But Arnold happens to be an exceptionally loyal person, and he wanted to stay with Munsingwear, if at all possible. So he asked me to try to negotiate a long-term licensing arrangement with the company for a line of Arnold Palmer autographed sportswear. This would have been a deal that could *breathe* – Munsingwear and Palmer would truly have been partners who benefited proportionately from the success of the line.

But Munsingwear stubbornly insisted on keeping things as they were. In the short run, it had a very sweet deal.

Meanwhile, not surprisingly, given the growth of golf and Arnold's phenomenal success on the pro tour, other offers kept coming in. Other companies were begging Palmer for exactly the sort of license deal that Munsingwear declined to enter into.

And this raises a point that I cannot stress too highly. In fact, as a service to all business people and all lawyers and all arbitrators and all mediators, I would like to paint this simple message across the sky:

LOPSIDED DEALS DON'T LAST

I must take a minute to expand on this point. False modesty aside, I have a reputation for being a tough and effective negotiator. I enjoy that reputation tremendously and needless to say, it helps me a great deal in my work.

However, I am sometimes astonished at the misunderstandings that surround the question of what being a good negotiator *means*.

Some people seem to think that negotiating means splitting the world up into Us and Them, getting as much as possible for Our side, and sticking it to the other guys at every opportunity.

That, in fact, is not negotiation; it's war.

Negotiation consists of devising means such that *all* sides feel they are profiting from a deal.

And not just profiting to some arbitrary degree, but *in accordance with fair market value in whatever arena they are operating.*

124

As long as no one was offering a better shake than Munsingwear, the Munsingwear deal was acceptable; as soon as offers worth ten or a hundred times more started cropping up, the Munsingwear deal had to adapt or it was doomed.

I sometimes see both business people and lawyers – especially young ones – come away from the negotiating table congratulating themselves for striking a bargain in which a clear disproportion of the benefits are on their side. They feel that they have been brilliant, they feel they have *won*.

Yet, in the great majority of cases, the victory will sour, and it will sour sooner rather than later.

There is virtually no such thing as a deal that can't be wriggled out of somehow or other. A corollary to that is:

McCormack's Axiom of Proportionate Wriggling

The more lopsided the contract, the greater the incentive for one side or the other to wriggle out of it.

The truly victorious negotiation, then, is one that leads to a deal with which all parties are happy *over time*.

In the Munsingwear situation, we were increasingly unhappy, and since the manufacturer was disinclined to bring the contract into line with market realities, we had no choice but to look for ways to end the deal.

We offered to buy our way out, but were turned down.

We made certain concessions in a possible licensing arrangement, but met with no interest.

So we went back to the contract in search of a fatal flaw such as overly rigid deals so often contain. And lo and behold, we found one.

In Arnold's contract there was a clause – presumably the brainchild of one of Munsingwear's bright young lawyers – which stipulated that the golfer would receive a bonus of $500 every time the penguin logo on his shirt appeared on national TV. Originally, this clause was designed to reward Arnold for golfing well enough to be in camera range during

125

those Saturday and Sunday telecasts when the tournament leaders were followed around the course.

However, in those years it was still legal for cigarettes to be advertised on TV, and in those years Palmer was still a smoker. Specifically, he smoked L & Ms, and Liggett and Myers, the manufacturer, was so pleased that it decided to make Arnold the star of a major ad campaign.

Now, the folks from L & M only cared about what Arnold smoked; it didn't matter to them what he *wore*. So why not do the commercials in a nice sport shirt with the penguin logo on it?

This would have resulted in many hundreds of 'bonusable' exposures on the tube, and it would have cost Munsingwear a great deal of money. It would, in fact, have cost Munsingwear *more* than we had been asking for a licensing deal, and they wouldn't even have got the benefit of a licence!

So they sheepishly changed their tune and let Arnold out of his contract after all.

If our lawyers deserve the credit for freeing our client from such a terrible deal, then Munsingwear's attorneys must bear the blame *for fashioning an arrangement that had no bend in it.*

In making a deal that was too good to be fair, they lost out on the possibility of a more mutually valuable arrangement in the longer term.

What's in the Black Box?

I hope I have managed to convey that the drawing up of contracts should really be thought of as an art form in which business people and lawyers collaborate. The business person forms the concept. The drafting lawyer gives it shape. Both should take credit for the beautiful artefact that results.

Contracts, however, are not the only aspect of business in which good communication between line executives and attorneys is essential. There are all sorts of areas in which one's own lawyers – in-house or outside counsel – provide services that are *advisory, cautionary or informative*.

To put it bluntly, there are times when lawyers not only are a pain in the neck, but *should* be.

Take the Black Box scenario as an example.

Since IMG is involved in conceiving, producing and marketing television sports programming, we get a fair number of unsolicited ideas – so-called Black Box items – sent to us by individuals who are convinced that they have dreamed up the catchiest show since *The Battle of the Network Stars*. These treasures generally arrive in envelopes marked 'Confidential'.

Are these ideas ever any good?

Don't ask me because I'm not allowed to look at them, and neither is anybody else!

I may be the boss, but my own legal department slams the Black Box shut in my face every time. They would be being derelict in their duties if they didn't.

The lawyers are painfully aware that if someone sends us an idea – notwithstanding that we didn't *ask* him to, and never mind that two hundred other people may have already had the same idea – and we *look* at his idea; and, at any time in the future, we produce a show that in any way *resembles* his idea, we may be subject to a claim that we misappropriated his idea.

This puts us in a bind.

First of all, television is a copycat medium. *Everything* on television resembles something else.

Second, it is at least *possible* that there will be a fabulous idea in one of those unsolicited envelopes – an idea that we would gladly pay for – but how will we know if we don't look inside, out of fear of provoking a claim?

Finally, there's a simple, basic fact of human nature to be dealt with: curiosity. How can you *resist* taking a peek?

In order to resist, you've got to *transcend ordinary human nature*.

This is what lawyers are not infrequently called upon to do; and *it is a very large part of why they can be so valuable to an organization*.

At moments when every fibre of a deal maker's being is crying out to look at that idea, the lawyer, like the disembodied voice of conscience, should yell out, DON'T DO IT.

This, you understand, is not necessarily a moral imperataive but a pragmatic one. Look inside an envelope marked 'Confidential' and you are asking to be sued.

If you are sued, regardless of the merits, you will almost certainly face a jury strongly biased in favour of the plaintiff.

Plaintiff's counsel will present the case as a righteous battle of a poor exploited individual against a big heartless company with deep pockets, and chances are the company will pay.

It is the lawyer's job to prevent all this from happening by making sure the company, like Caesar's wife, is *not just free of blame but above suspicion.*

In order to do this, IMG's staff attorneys have instituted procedures about as complicated as – but let's hope more effective than – Pentagon security measures. We have locked files. We return unopened letters by registered mail, double-sealed with metal tape. We get affidavits, waivers and releases before we will even *talk* to someone.

If these measures seem extreme, they are. But they are necessary.

And the point I want to make is one that is too often underappreciated by business people. **There truly are situations where there is no substitute for the formality, fastidiousness, and even finickiness that lawyers bring to a problem.**

Anything short of these attributes can spell disaster, and that's the terrible truth.

See What I Mean?

In case you think I'm exaggerating the sensitivity of Black Box issues, let me pass along the story of one of the strangest episodes our company ever had the misfortune to be involved in.

A few years ago, IMG's television production subsidiary, TWI, was sued by an individual who had submitted to us, unsolicited, a film treatment whose working title was *The Muscleless Wonder.* Suffice it to say that we were interested neither in acquiring nor developing this opus.

At around the same time, however, TWI was preparing to make a TV movie from an adaptation of a novel called

Addison. The plaintiff claimed that *his* treatment was in fact the germ from which our screenplay had sprung.

There were only three small flaws in this resourceful and, on the face of it, not unreasonable argument:

1. We hadn't read this fellow's treatment.
2. The adaptation of *Addison* had been done before *The Muscleless Wonder* was even received.
3. There was virtually no resemblance between the two stories.

The plaintiff in this case, who was not a lawyer, decided he would represent himself. Whether this decision was strategic or economic we will never know.

In any event, *his* legal costs were virtually nil, while we, of course, had to assign one of our staff lawyers to deal with the suit in a responsible manner. She had to answer documents, make several trips to New York, and so forth.

Eventually, the suit was thrown out. We had 'won' — though, given the quirks of the American legal system, we had no way of recovering the expenses we should never have had to shell out in the first place.

That, however, was not quite the end of the story. The plaintiff ended up in the penitentiary, and while there he wrote us three or four letters a week, still claiming that we had stolen his brainchild. We hear from him occasionally to this very day.

With such people around, it's a damn good thing that lawyers take every precaution!

Reports from the Front

Most business people, if they are reasonably bright and if they pay attention, will pick up a fair amount of knowledge of the law, as it pertains to their businesses, by osmosis.

If the law stayed still, chances are most people would know about as much as they needed to by the time they had risen to positions of real responsibility within their companies.

For better or worse, however, the law *doesn't* stay still.

129

It's constantly changing, and, as with so many things in our society, the rate at which it changes seems to be accelerating all the time.

A friend of mine who has been practising law for many years tells me that there was a time when one referred either to the tax code of 1939 or the one from 1954.

Then there were yearly revisions.

Then monthly supplements were added.

Today there are data bases available that feature new information *hourly*.

In antitrust, in liability, even in divorce and child-custody cases, the law has been evolving at an even-faster clip – far faster than any business person could keep abreast of, given that most of his or her time and energy is taken up with other things.

One of the key functions that attorneys perform for business people, then, is to issue reports from the legal front.

As with any aspect of legal service, this role can be performed well or it can be performed badly. *Any* lawyer can spend his working hours poring over journals and government notices, then write pompous-sounding memos informing the staff that the wording of such and such a statute has been changed.

That's the flat *minimum* a lawyer should do, and it's of only very limited use to the people on the business side.

What an attorney *ought* to do is report not just on the changes in the law, but on the *applications and implications* of those changes.

Footprints on the Earth

Let me illustrate. Our company, in its role as a producer of television programming, regularly negotiates deals for the use of that programming. Traditionally, these deals have been made on a country-by-country or, occasionally, a continent-by-continent basis. As long as the programmes were broadcast by conventional means, it was fairly simple and straightforward to say, 'You can air this programme in France, but

130

not in Belgium,' or 'Your rights to this material end at the Canadian border.'

What happens, however, when broadcasts are sent by satellite – a new technology that has nothing to do with national boundaries and, in itself, is subject only to physical laws?

As a matter of earthly jurisprudence, the rules governing the use of satellite broadcasting are still being hashed out. And one of the jobs of our in-house counsel is to keep us informed of what is going on at that busy intersection where law collides with technology – and also collides with the bottom line.

Quite often, we sell sports programming to the cable network ESPN. When we do, we take the stance that ESPN is buying the rights to broadcast in the United States, its territories and possessions. ESPN, however, takes the position that it's buying the rights to use the shows throughout what is known as the network's 'footprint'.

A footprint is the entire sweep of earth that is within reach of a given satellite's signals. The ESPN footprint happens to include a fair amount of Central America, South America and Canada – markets which traditionally would all be sold separately.

In terms of established practice in broadcasting, then, we feel that our position is absolutely justified, and that ESPN is trying to get more for its money than is fair. But even if we win the battle to limit ESPN's broadcast territory, we still have the problem posed by the 'new territory', i.e., the satellite. What happens is that ESPN tells these 'footprint' territories that they cannot show the programming in question. But, in fact, it is right up there in the sky, available to them. Do they honour the ESPN instruction, or do they simply show it anyway?

The real answer is, most of the time we don't know. Many of these territories are small, distant, and difficult to check on. And suppose we find out they did violate ESPN's instructions; whom do we sue? ESPN? The territory? And for how much?

International law on this subject is mostly unwritten as yet. So our deal people continue to argue and monitor the law.

131

Closer to Home

Not that the lawyers' role as advance scouts pertains only to such exotic subjects as high tech.

In more down-to-earth ways as well, **a company's attorneys should keep the line executives meaningfully informed on shifts in the legal climate.**

Take endorsements. They are obviously a tremendous income source for the athletes we represent, and advising our clients on what products and services to endorse is an integral part of the service we provide.

Giving this advice responsibly is more complicated than you might imagine, however, because *every endorsement carries with it a potential liability*.

And as our legal system becomes more and more liberal in its interpretation of liability, dangers crop up, like rocks at low tide, where none had been seen before.

Thrown for a Loss

A couple of years ago, for example, Johnny Unitas, formerly the great quarterback for the Baltimore Colts, was sued by two men who had lost money in an investment firm that Unitas had endorsed and that had turned out to be a fraud.

The company, First Fidelity Financial Services, went belly-up, and its founder was indicted on eight felony counts.

Unitas himself had had nothing whatsoever to do with the scam. His sole connection with First Fidelity was that he had accepted a fee of $7000 for doing some radio and newspaper ads on behalf of the company.

The grounds on which he was sued were actually very touching, though legally shaky. The plaintiff's attorney argued, essentially, that *everybody trusted Johnny U.*, and that, even if he was not guilty of any wrongdoing, he had a responsibility to check more closely into the soundness of the product he was endorsing.

Johnny Unitas was not a client of ours, and, except for newspaper coverage in Baltimore and some very spotty mentions elsewhere, this case actually received only a little publicity. Nevertheless, IMG's legal staff followed it closely, as it had clear implications for people who *were* our clients.

As soon as the suit was filed, our general counsel, Bill Carpenter, started sending us memos about the issues it raised. He went beyond the Unitas affair, to review for us certain low points in the history of celebrity or 'expert' endorsements.

In 1978, for example, singer Pat Boone had been hit with a suit for endorsing an acne medicine that didn't work and that had dangerous side effects. The lessons to be drawn from that débâcle were writ large in Carpenter's memos: beware of endorsing anything used on the body, and, for God's sake, don't claim that you or your family actually *use* the product if you don't.

In 1985 Dr Barry Bricklin was subject to a complaint by the Federal Trade Commission because of his endorsement of the so-called 'Rotation diet'. The FTC ruled that Bricklin 'knew or should have known' that the diet's promised weight loss was a gross exaggeration.

The crucial phrase here, of course, was '*should have known*'. As Carpenter pointed out, this suggested that, when endorsing something as an expert, or in a field in which one could be *construed* to be an expert, the endorser should review not just the ads, but the *evidence* on which the ads were purportedly based.

The Unitas case raised red flags of its own. Celebrity athletes are quite regularly asked to lend their names and likenesses to various financial services, and financial services routinely make rather optimistic claims about anticipated rates of return.

What if a financial service, even in the absence of fraud, failed to perform as claimed? What if John Madden, say, were paid to stand in front of a new condo development and say it was a fantastic investment as well as a great place to live, and as an investment the development turned out to be a dog? Where exactly does an endorser's liability begin and end, so far as investors' money is concerned?

How much is an endorser required to know – or for that

matter *care* – about a product he or she is very obviously being *paid* to endorse?

As it happened, Johnny Unitas's attorneys successfully argued that he could not be held accountable for the misdeeds of First Fidelity's principals.

But the point here is that, by paying close attention to the case, and by *interpreting it in ways that were meaningful to our business*, our lawyers made our line executives a bit more informed and more sophisticated in the matter of endorsements.

They answered questions for us that we might not even have thought to ask.

They made us better at our jobs.

And that, finally, is what playing as a team is all about.

7

Things I Wish Every Lawyer Knew

The two preceding chapters have been about the two sides of McCormack's Central Paradox about businessmen and lawyers:

Businessmen and lawyers tend to have deep temperamental differences that make conflict between them almost inevitable.

However, by viewing those differences not in terms of conflict but of mutual advantage, both sides can advance their interests.

They can mould themselves into a team that is more powerful and versatile than any single player.

Knowing Each Other's Moves

Playing as a team, however, requires unanimity of effort. Achieving that unanimity is our subject now.

I'm reminded of the way that Paul Hornung and Jim Taylor used to block for each other back in the glory days of the Green Bay Packers.

Hornung and Taylor moved so well together that every cut and feint seemed to have been choreographed. It didn't look like the runner was following the blocker; the zigs and zags were too spontaneous for that. Rather, it seemed as if the blocker was somehow seeing the runner with eyes in the back of his head. That's how well they *knew each other's moves*.

And that, I think, is the key phrase here.

For a lawyer and a client to get the best results, each should know the other's style, abilities and limitations.

Each should know the other's goals and priorities.

Each should understand what motivates the other, the sorts of challenges that get the juices flowing, the things that make the other lose interest or lose heart.

And each should know what makes the other mad.

Some Like It Short

Let's start with the things that make me the maddest: wasted time, effort and verbiage.

A number of years ago, our company was approached by a leading NHL hockey player who wanted us to represent him, and whom we would have been very pleased to have as a client.

There was only one small problem: the athlete was already under contract to another agent.

But he was very unhappy with that arrangement, and wanted our help in getting out of it.

So I asked to see his current contract. He reached into his attaché case, and of course I expected him to produce the typical five- or ten- or forty-page document.

Instead, he handed over a single sheet of paper. My first response was: great, no problem. How serious a commitment could possibly be indicated by four or five lines of longhand?

The thing didn't even *look* like a contract. All it said, in paraphrase, was that 'I, ----, hereby agree that the XYZ Agency can represent me exclusively with respect to my business activities throughout the world for a period of five years beginning 1 January, 19--, and that I will pay a commission of 25 per cent of my gross income for this service.' Period.

I passed the contract along to our legal department, asking their advice as to how the agreement might be voided.

They told me there was no way it could be. The contract was perfectly legitimate, binding, and about as airtight as any contract ever is.

This bit of news had two consequences. The first, of course, was that we could not represent this particular athlete.

The second was that I wondered why, if this haiku held up fine under legal scrutiny, it was impossible for *me* ever to get anything so short and concise out of *my* lawyers.

That, as I said, was some years ago, and I'm *still* wondering!

Processes and Results

This seeming impossibility of getting anything *short and fast* out of a lawyer drives me, and I think most business people, crazy. It is one of the central truisms of our culture that business people are chronically – and sometimes comically – pressed for time.

Executives are always running to catch planes or putting abrupt endings to phone calls so that they can move on to other phone calls.

Business letters are notoriously terse and clipped, often at the expense of both grammar and graciousness.

For all that, when lawyers draft documents that require a business person's attention, they act as if their clients had all the time in the world to wade through them. The terrible truth is that lawyers tend not just to be thorough but obsessive.

Why?

The answer has to do with something that *is* taught at law school.

Law schools teach that everything is a *process* – a *chain* of reasoning with a *series* of causes and effects.

Well, that's fine, but business people are generally less interested in the twists and turns than in the *conclusions* – not the process but the *result*.

So, one of the things I wish all lawyers were aware of is that they can spare me the details of their brilliant logical pirouettes *and just tell me what's going on*!

Easy on the Adjectives

And while we're at it, I wish that lawyers would throw away their thesauruses.

137

Consider this gem of legal draftsmanship, taken from our files, pertaining to a suit brought against us in 1983, and which, in spite of all the sound and fury, came to nothing:

> . . . defendant IMG did wrongfully, knowingly, intentionally, wantonly, maliciously, and without reasonable justification or excuse, induce, persuade, and entice the defendant BAT and/or ITF and/or IMG to violate, repudiate, and break the said contract with plaintiff . . .

What is this fellow talking about and whom is he trying to impress? This ponderous paragraph does nothing more than claim that we broke the contract. *So why not say it that way?*

I think I speak for most clients when I say that I don't hire a lawyer to be impressed by his vocabulary.

A lawyer may *imagine* he's making a big hit with his Latin phrases and five-syllable words, but in fact I'm likely to be tapping my foot and stealing glances at my watch as he holds forth.

I'm also likely to be resentful of the money *I'm* spending so that he can indulge his verbosity!

Let's face it: most of the grand rhetorical flourishes aren't really an integral part of lawyering; they're just a way of showing off.

Playing to the Crowd

Not that drafting is the only area in which lawyers tend to indulge in bravado.

In meetings, too, they sometimes seem less concerned with substantive results than with turning in a flashy performance.

A few years ago, I was negotiating with one of the networks for the US television rights to a major sports championship. At the first bargaining session, the network's head of sports programming brought along his chief of business affairs (who was an MBA) and a pair of lawyers.

About five minutes into the meeting, it became patently clear that all of us were wasting our time. The head of sports

138

progamming – the real decision maker – was being perfectly reasonable. But the head of business affairs was determined to show how tough he could be. He rolled up his shirt sleeves, planted his elbows on the mahogany table, and set out to impress his boss by taking the stance that he would make no financial concessions, reasonable or otherwise.

Well, the lawyers couldn't very well let themselves be outdone by the MBA, could they? They were *there*, after all; they had to make a 'contribution'.

So they tried not only to be cleverer, tougher and more intransigent than the head of business, but also more dogged than *each other*.

It got to the point where I felt **the actual subject of the negotiation had virtually ceased to matter; what was going on was simply some unpleasant and unproductive ritual among the members of the other side's 'team'.**

I quickly found a pretext for cutting the meeting short.

Some time thereafter, I phoned the head of sports programming and told him I had a couple of ideas I wanted to discuss with him.

We got together, just the two of us, and within an hour and a half we had hammered out the basic points of a mutually advantageous deal — acceptable enough to all concerned so that both sides have happily stayed together for over ten years.

Why was it so much easier to get the deal done tête-à-tête?

The issues were the same, and my opposite number and I were equally intent on not giving away the store.

The crucial difference was that **we were talking to each other, rather than playing to the crowd.**

We didn't need to grandstand because we realized something that I wish more lawyers would realize. **The evidence that we had done our job existed in the deal itself, not in the posturing and one-upmanship we had indulged in to get it done.**

Now the Positive Side

So far in this chapter I have been giving vent to a few pet peeves – things I wish lawyers knew *not* to do.

But the other side of the coin – the positive side – is even more important.

I *do* wish lawyers would be less theoretical and more pragmatic.

I wish, for example, that more lawyers would approach negotiation *as a business person approaches it*; that is, not as a rigid and formal process, but as **an elaborate game that involves creativity, close attention to human nature, improvisation, and sometimes, to be perfectly candid, such tactics as bluffing and manipulation.**

This game has only two rules:

1. *Everything* is negotiable.
2. *Anything* can be used as a tool in a negotiation.

A Yen for Profits

Even such seemingly extraneous elements as currency considerations can become, under certain circumstances, valuable bargaining chips.

Anyone who does business in a multinational context is well aware of the impact that currency fluctuations can have on profits. But I wonder how many people *use* currency issues effectively.

A couple of years ago, a licensing contract between Bjorn Borg and a leading Japanese knitwear manufacturer came up for renewal.

The Japanese company, whose profits had been declining, hadn't done as well with this line of products as it had hoped to, and came to the bargaining table seeking a reduction in the main guarantee that Bjorn was to receive.

Our position was that our client had more than lived up to his obligations, and that, now that he was a known quantity in terms of cooperation and availability, his guarantee should increase. The company's profits, we argued, would certainly increase in the near future.

How could these two positions be reconciled?

The company, of course, did most of its business in yen. Its contract with us was in dollars. And the yen had recently appreciated substantially against the dollar.

By staying keenly attuned to the currency fluctuations – *as well as to their psychological effects* – we were able to reach an agreement that made the manufacturers happy because it cost fewer yen, and made our client happy because it gave him more dollars!

And we built goodwill for IMG on both sides because it seemed to the casual observer that we had pulled the money out of a hat.

The Match Game

A crucial and often dramatic sort of negotiation that we have not yet had occasion to discuss features *competitive bidding*. And I wish lawyers knew more about the special psychology that pertains when bidders go head-to-head.

As anyone who has ever attended any sort of auction will testify, there are few scenarios more likely to elicit fireworks than the one in which two or more people want the same item, and at least one of them isn't going to get it!

In auction situations, rationality battles with passion, and the business imperative to buy *at the right price* contends with the more primitive impulse *not to lose at any price*.

At IMG over the years, we have participated in all sorts of 'match game' situations – both as auctioneers and as bidders. Experience has taught us a couple of things that all lawyers and negotiators should keep in mind:

1. Never underestimate the role of *theatre* in an auction, and never pass up opportunities to raise the stakes by dramatic staging.

2. Don't let the single issue of money squeeze you into an overly 'linear' approach to competitive bidding. Winning bids are often those that manage to sweeten the deal in non-monetary ways.

By way of illustrating point number one above, let me tell you about what was probably the most dramatic auction we have ever been involved with.

This concerned the US television rights for the 1988 Winter Olympics, and the numbers were simply enormous. Our client, the Organizing Committee for the Calgary Games, had trusted our advice on how to conduct the bidding, and it was decided to create as much suspense as possible.

We drafted a contract that included all provisions *except those having to do with rights money.*

We then submitted that contract to *all three American networks.* In order to indicate their acceptance of the non-monetary terms and, indeed, to qualify to bid for the games, they were to sign the documents, without the money provisions.

The IOC then asked them to meet in Lausanne, Switzerland, to fill in the final blanks and to see which network's contract would be completed and which remaining two would be discarded.

Why Lausanne?

Well, the International Olympic Committee is headquartered there, and that fitted perfectly into the crafted intrigue: there's nothing like a transoceanic plane ride to let the suspense build up and to underscore that the stakes are high. And besides, *doesn't everybody spend more when they're travelling?*

Prior to our arrival in Lausanne, we entrusted much of the drafting and negotiating strategy to one of our staff attorneys who happens to be a woman. Now, most of the people in our business are fairly progressive and enlightened, but still, sports has traditionally been a male bastion, and some males get a little nonplussed at the active presence of a woman in the proverbial smoke-filled room. This particular woman, Betsy Goff, is nearly six feet tall, totally poised, ultraprofessional, and as tough a negotiator as we have.

Did it bother us that some of our bidders might be nonplussed? You bet it didn't.

What, in the end, did all our dramatics and choreography add up to? A rights fee of $309,000,000, $96,000,000 *more* than was predicted would be bid the day we arrived in Lausanne.

So, if you're ever going to stage an auction, think Broadway.

The Deal the Other Side Can't Match

If you're sitting in an auction room at Sotheby's, bidding for a vase, obviously the only factor under your control is the amount of money you're willing to spend.

You can't explain to the auctioneer how beautifully you would display the vase, or argue that you would care for it better than anyone else. A Sotheby auction doesn't work that way.

But *some* kinds of auctions *do*. And lawyers, as well as *all* negotiators who are involved in a bidding situation, should be aware that sometimes the crucial determinant is not the money, but something you can offer and the other side can't.

A number of years ago, the National Basketball Association, which we represented, was due to renew its television contract. Barry Frank, the head of sales of our television subsidiary, TWI, was spearheading the transaction for the league, and he opened the floor to bids.

Now, NBA games had long been aired by ABC, and ABC wanted to keep it that way. In dollar amounts, the network was prepared to match virtually any offer.

But some of the league owners preferred to switch to CBS, so the NBA Television Committee came up with a masterstroke that nearly short-circuited the purely linear approach. They convinced CBS, which also badly wanted the NBA contract, to air a certain number of games on Saturday afternoons in the fall of the year, and argued that this particular form of increased exposure to the sports audience would be of great long-term benefit to pro basketball.

The promise of Saturday afternoon air time was one that ABC *could not possibly match*, because of a longstanding commitment to televise college football.

So CBS got the contract.

And ABC sued, claiming that the 'Saturday afternoons in the fall' clause had been contrived *specifically* as a provision they couldn't match, and that therefore ABC had been unlawfully deprived of its right of refusal on the pact.

Now, this was an interesting lawsuit, because everybody within the sports industry *knew* that CBS's gambit had been *precisely* designed to ace out ABC. It couldn't have been more obvious.

On the other hand, however, the judge who heard the case ruled that Saturday exposure *did* add value to the league – and therefore CBS won the case, and airs pro basketball to this very day.

The moral of the story is look for values *other than money* that can tip the scales in your favour.

Myself on the Block

Let me round out this brief accounting of competitive-bidding tactics with a story about the sale of my first book, which dealt with things you don't learn at Harvard Business School.

We decided to put this book up for auction, and several publishers made bids. In exchange for certain considerations, Bantam Books was given the 'floor' – i.e., the right to match any other offer that came in.

The bidding escalated, and everyone dropped out except Bantam and William Morrow.

At this point, Morrow came up with what seemed a brilliant ploy, in keeping with the idea of the offer that can't be matched: it suggested paying us an exorbitant royalty on paperback sales, a percentage dramatically higher than industry norms.

Why?

Because Morrow, essentially a hardcover house, didn't especially *care* about paperback sales. In theory, it would make its money before a paperback even came out.

Bantam, on the other hand, was *perceived* as basically a paperback house – which of course is what it traditionally had been. If Bantam was thinking of the Harvard book mainly as a paperback, the jumbo royalty would pose two problems: it would force the publishers to set a dangerous precedent as to how much they would pay, and it would make it very tough for them to turn a profit on the book.

Unbeknown to anyone at the time, however, Bantam was on the brink of a major strategic repositioning: and was about to become a major player in the hardcover game.

So, to the surprise not only of Morrow's lawyers but of us as well, Bantam did match the offer and got the book.

Which leads me to this cautionary note: if you're going to pin your hopes on a supposedly unmatchable proposition, make sure it *is* in fact unmatchable.

First Win the War, then Fight the Skirmishes

A publishing saga doesn't end with the awarding of the contract, however, and the story of the Harvard book deal has other chapters germane to our discussion.

At law school they teach you that a contract, once signed, is binding and immutable – unless formally altered by a subsequent contract. This concept in law is so basic as to be almost sacred, and it's no coincidence that 'the sanctity of contracts' is such an often-heard cliché.

But business people realize – and lawyers *should* realize – that in practice matters are much more fluid. A contract reflects an understanding. And understandings between humans are usually imperfect. They often need revising.

In the case of the Harvard book, what happened was this: Bantam published the book in hardcover form, and I'm happy to say it was quite successful. The publishers and I both more than recovered our investment of time, trouble and money.

When it came time to publish the paperback edition, however, Bantam informed me that it couldn't do so under the terms we'd originally agreed to. As we knew all along, it would be virtually impossible for the publishers to make money under the original contract's royalty provision. *Now* they wanted to renegotiate.

I *could* have got angry. I could even have accused Bantam of negotiating in bad faith in the first place. However, a number of things prevented my reacting that way:

1.   There wasn't anyone around to be mad at. Jack Romanos, the man who had made the original deal, had left Bantam and gone to Simon and Schuster. His successors claimed – fairly – that it wasn't *their* fault they had been saddled with a no-win contract.

Lawyers should understand that, *in practice, these shifts of personnel happen all the time, and while they can be troublesome, they also provide useful pretexts for renegotiating contracts, throwing out contracts, and giving people various ways of saving face.*

2.   Bantam was probably not going to publish a paperback anyway, but there was something to be gained by being sympathetic towards their position. The publishers felt they could renegotiate with me because they judged – correctly – that *I* wanted the paperback to be published soon, and with as much enthusiasm as the hardcover had been. Ultimately, they got the relief they were looking for, and we both got a successful paperback.

3.   In their position, *I probably would have done exactly the same*, in keepng with a philosophy that I wish all attorneys and negotiators would take to heart:

First win the war; then worry about the little battles.

First get the contract; then see if you can live with it.

It's Not As Bad As It Sounds

I realize that sounds rather cynical, so let me explain it a bit.

I'm not saying one should take contract provisions lightly, and I'm certainly not advocating making agreements that one doesn't intend to honour.

146

I *am* saying, however, that in any deal there's the Big Picture, and then there are the Small Details.

At law school they teach you that *every syllable of a contract is equally important.*

In theory, that's true.

In practice, it's nonsense.

The Big Picture is what matters, and the rest is usually nickels and dimes.

Just recently, we were approached by a major corporation on behalf of our new client, America's Cup winner Dennis Conner. The customer was very keen on getting Conner to do a number of speaking engagements for them, but they weren't yet firm on the dates or locations of the speeches involved.

Now, Dennis is a very busy man these days, and he's also a very scrupulous one. His initial response was to turn down the offer because he felt there was a good chance there would be a conflict or two along the way, and he probably wouldn't be able to fulfil all the dates that were being asked of him.

We counselled him to sign the contract and then take the events case by case.

Does this make us bad?

The answer has to do with the question of intent. We certainly didn't intend to mislead the customer. Rather, we intended to make them happy *most* of the time.

If Dennis Conner can give them what they want on thirty-five occasions and has to disappoint them on the thirty-sixth, business people will understand.

And lawyers, too, should understand that all the black-and-white contracts in the world can't eliminate the shades of grey that represent how deals *really* work.

The Best Defence Is a Good Offence

As we have seen, competitive bidding is a dicey business from the perspective of the bidder. In the heat of battle, prices get jacked up and impulsive promises get made. And a lot of the time, after all the trouble and expense of putting in a bid, you go home empty-handed anyway.

But what if there were a way of *avoiding* bidding situations?

In fact, there is a way – though too few lawyers take advantage of it.

The way is to **be creative about renewing contracts.**

Obviously, a current contract holder generally has an inside track on a new negotiation. If nothing else, the person often has a first-refusal clause or some other sort of option provision.

What he *also* has, however, and what is really more important, is *the rights holder's ear.* He can talk to the rights holder at any time – and can discuss renewal at any point.

How do most attorneys handle renewal procedures?

The terrible truth is: stupidly.

All they do is flag a file to remind them when a contract is three or six months away from expiring.

Of course, *the people who lost the bidding the last time around are doing exactly the same thing*! So right away you're off to the races again: another time-consuming and expensive auction.

Why not renew *sooner*? And at a time when everybody is *thrilled* with the relationship?

This was a stratagem employed with great success by ABC back in the 1970s, when that network was very aggressively seeking to become the pre-eminent force in sports programming.

Let's say that back in 1975 the rights to a very attractive athletic event were being auctioned off. At that point, ABC would have had no choice but to bid head-to-head against the other two networks. If ABC offered the best deal – as it often did in those high-flying years – that network might walk away from the table with a contract to air the event for five seasons.

CBS and NBC, meanwhile, having lost in the bidding, would put memos in their follow-up files to contact the rights holder in 1979, and try once again to secure the event for themselves.

What the other networks would often find, however, was that by the time 1979 rolled around, ABC had already renewed for several more years!

Typically, ABC would set about renewing two or three years into a five-year contract. The network would say to the rights holder, 'Look, we're doing well with this arrangement and so are you. Let's negotiate an increase in your payments for the remaining years on the contract, and extend it three or four years into the future.'

Now think about the psychology of this offer. First of all, it makes the point man for the rights holder – the head of one of the amateur sports federations, say – look awfully good. He can go to his board and impress them with the way he 'got' ABC to alter an existing arrangement to the benefit of their organization.

Second, since these sorts of people are fond of erecting monuments to themselves, the rights holder is likely to want to extend the deal so as to increase the lifespan of his legacy.

Further, by jumping the gun on the expected renewal time, chances are that ABC will be able to negotiate unilaterally without the other networks even knowing what's in the works. Should CBS and NBC become aware of the renewal negotiations, will they be likely to allocate money for a project that couldn't become effective for several years anyway?

For all those reasons, the aggressive approach taken by ABC's lawyers and producers gave the network a real leg up against adversaries who simply did things by the book.

One Year Times Five or Five Years Times One?

Analogous to the psychology involved in renewing contracts is the psychology that should be used in shaping termination language.

As I mentioned earlier with regard to the Australian Termination Clause, the wording of a contract-ending provision can go a long way towards determining if a contract is ended or not.

On the surface, for example, it might seem that there is no

difference between a one-year contract with an option to continue for five years, and a five-year contract with an option to terminate after one year.

I believe very strongly that in fact there are significant differences between the two — differences that hinge entirely on human psychology. And I wish more lawyers were more attuned to those psychological resonances.

Let's say that Chris Schenkel has a contract as spokesman for Eastern Airlines, and that the contract is for one year, with Eastern having the option to extend.

Psychologically speaking, it will be very easy for the airline *passively* to cancel the arrangement, just by letting the option date go by and doing nothing.

No confrontations will be necessary, no one's ego will be put on the line or bruised. Unless everyone is absolutely thrilled with the deal, there's a real chance it will just fall through a crack. Ending the relationship will be as easy as *not* making a phone call.

If, on the other hand, the contract is for five years, with Eastern having the option not to extend but to *terminate it*, the airline has to take an *active* stance if it wants out. It has to make a *positive* decision to end the arrangement. Most daunting of all, someone has to go to Chris and say, in effect, 'We don't want you any more.'

This is a hard thing for almost anyone to say, especially since there will certainly be personal relationships between Schenkel and the Eastern executives by the time the option comes up.

In practice, then, **the sheer interpersonal discomfort of terminating the contract becomes a real incentive to keep the agreement in force – and to make the agreement work to the benefit of both sides.**

Can Insurance Be Creative?

As everybody in business already knows, there is a bad insurance crisis brewing around the world, and especially in America. Sky-rocketing premiums, shrinking coverage, whimsical cancellations – these are problems on which whole books have already been written.

For our purposes here, however, I would just like to make a couple of points about insurance that too few people – and too few lawyers – seem to think about.

Most people view insurance as, well, *insurance* – a hedge against worst-case possibilities, but certainly *not* a source of profit.

However, why *shouldn't* insurance be a revenue centre? It certainly is for the insurers!

Often when a promoter puts on a tennis championship, for example, he is actually playing two distinct roles. He can make or lose money from the gate and sale of broadcast rights. He can also make or lose money based on the performance of the top-seeded star players.

A tournament promoter routinely buys rainout insurance. If the promoter's star players get knocked out in the early rounds, the promoter will very often make less money if the finals are played as scheduled than if they are rained out.

I am sure that a lot of promoters have spent more than one Saturday evening praying for thunderstorms!

A couple of years ago, we contracted to stage a series of three races between the great English milers Steve Ovett and Sebastian Coe. We insured the race-readiness of both runners, since obviously there would be no event unless both were fit.

To cut a long story short, first Coe pulled a hamstring, then Ovett bruised a heel, and then Coe pulled a hamstring again.

No races were run, but we recovered the lost income from the insurers.

Insuring the Pope

The point, however, is not to insure yourself to the eyeballs and then wait for disaster to make you rich.

Rather, the idea is to be so heads-up about insurance that you will come out all right *no matter what*.

In this connection, I would like to tell you about probably

the most complex and sophisticated insurance matter we ever had to deal with.

In 1980, we were approached by the English Catholic Church and the Vatican to represent the commercial aspects of Pope John Paul II's impending visit to Great Britain, which was to take place about eighteen months later in the summer of 1982. The problem was that when the Pope had visited Ireland several years earlier to perform a Mass before over a million worshippers, the visit ended up costing the Catholic Church and the Vatican about two million pounds. This resulted from the high costs of setting up a sound system, security systems, hospital and sanitation facilites, etc., for the multitudes, and also from the high costs of air, helicopter and ground transportation.

What disturbed the Vatican representatives, however, was that when they arrived, they found countless people were going through the crowds before, during, and after the Mass selling everything from T-shirts to religious items to sand-wiches. The Catholic Church had two major problems with this. The first was that the quality of the items was generally poor, and the second problem was that none of the proceeds from the sales went to the Church to help defray the cost of the visit.

We had a couple of discussions with the English Catholic Church and Vatican representatives, which resulted in IMG representing the commercial elements of the papal visit, the development and trademarking of papal logos, the supervision of product quality, and the negotiation of a great number of licensing arrangements for 'official products of the Papal Tour'.

This activity was handled by Ian Todd, who is our senior marketing executive in Britain and Europe, and a qualified lawyer as well as an effective salesman.

Everything about the papal visit was enormously com-plicated – the security, the transportation, the media access, and the licensing arrangements for dozens of endorsed products.

Not the least bedevilling problem was what would happen

if the Pope, because of illness, political problems, or whatever, was unable to perform one or more of the six scheduled outdoor Masses? These Masses were the main rationale for the Pope's trip. Hundreds of thousands of people would attend, and presumably millions of dollars of products *might* be sold. Clearly, we needed insurance coverage for the Pope's appearances.

But obviously no such policy existed in ready-made form!

So Ian Todd had to write one. This, in turn, raises a point that every attorney and business person should be aware of: insurance companies would like you to think that their policies are carved in stone, and all that's left for you to do is fill in the blanks.

That's nonsense. There's no reason why an insurance policy can't be drafted from scratch, just like any other contract. And there's no reason why each and every clause in it shouldn't be negotiable.

In drafting this unique policy for the Pope, Ian Todd had a very important priority in mind. He wanted to avoid the usual procedure of first filing a claim, then having to establish the dollar amount of the loss. There would be no precedent to follow if, say, a Mass had to be cancelled because of a storm, and so how could damages be fairly assessed?

To solve the problem, Ian did *exhaustive* research *before* drafting the policy. By the time he went to the insurers, he could tell them *precisely* how many worshippers were expected at each stop on the tour, how many articles were expected to be sold, and so forth. His figures were so detailed that he was able to get the insurance company to *spell out and guarantee* payments on almost any contingency.

As it happened, the Pope did celebrate six Masses. However, the venue of one of them was changed.

Our insurance policy was so clear and explicit that we had a mathematical formula for determining exactly how much we had lost by the switch in plan! We collected just over $100,000 on the Vatican's behalf, and saved ourselves the time, trouble, and possible conflicts of having to establish a claim after the fact.

Insurance is one way of dealing with the hard fact that things don't always turn out exactly as planned.

Another way of dealing with things that don't quite pan out is letting the other side off the hook.

There are a surprising number of occasions on which one may apply the following axiom:

McCormack's Axiom of Good Pragmatic Deeds

Sometimes there is more money to be made from letting people out of contracts than by holding them to commitments that are disadvantageous to them.

I'm not talking, of course, about cases in which the other party has shown bad faith or has got into a bind because of their own incompetence. In such instances, we just shrug and collect our money.

But sometimes, let's face it, things happen that just could not have been foreseen.

Let's say, for example, that the Donnay racquet company enters into a five-year contract with Bjorn Borg to endorse a line of wooden racquets. Two years into the contract, everyone starts playing with graphite and composite racquets, and wooden racquets of every manufacture are piling up in warehouses.

Strictly speaking, this is not our problem. Donnay owes us three more years of fees.

But at the time we made the deal, everyone thought a wooden racquet with Borg's signature would sell. The people at Donnay who made that judgement are no doubt feeling pretty bad; maybe their jobs are in jeopardy. Borg, of course, would like to do business with Donnay in the future.

So, if we agree to cancel their obligation, the executives are off the hook, they will feel that they owe analogous consideration in the future, and chances are they will bend over backwards to deal with us again.

This obviously is a *business* judgement, not a legal one, and lawyers sometimes have a tough time understanding it. Yale or Harvard or East Podunk Law School had taught them to work very hard at fashioning contracts that are as complete and as watertight as possible; it's hard for them not to feel subverted if the business side just decides to throw out the contract.

But I would argue that attorneys sometimes become so fixated on the solidity of their contracts that they lose sight of what the ultimate *purpose* of the contract really is.

The ultimate purpose of any contract is not to get a stranglehold on the other party, but to formalize an understanding that is of real and proportionate benefit to both sides over time.

When You Can't Deliver the Goods

Just as we have occasionally released business partners from obligations they couldn't reasonably fulfil, so now and then we have elected to give a refund where circumstances prevented us from doing the kind of job we like to do.

This is difficult for several reasons.

First of all, it obviously costs the company money.

Second, no one likes to admit he fell short of meeting the task.

But my contention is that **dignity and goodwill are better served by freely acknowledging when you just can't deliver the goods.**

Several years ago, we arranged for Levi Strauss to sponsor a computerized ranking service for joggers. The idea was a very ambitious one that promised to give Levi's a great grass-roots exposure that would be totally appropriate to the company's image.

The plan basically was this. If you were, say, a thirty-five-year-old female who had run a half-dozen 10K races at an average time of forty-seven minutes, you would file that information with the Levi's Runners Ranking Service, and receive a computer ranking by age, gender, geographical area, and so forth. This information, in turn, could be used to qualify you for other races, or just to let you know where you stood.

As the saying goes, it looked good on paper, but it didn't really fly. There were some organizational problems. Creating national awareness of the ranking service was enormously difficult. Worst of all, the runners themselves were either intimidated by the computer or just didn't want to bother filling in the forms.

So IMG found itself in a position where legally it had done everything it was obligated to do, and more; yet we knew very well that the sponsor wasn't getting value for money.

We could have kept our fees and said sorry – but that's a no-class way to do business. So we gave a lot of the money back – and I believe we have a friend in San Francisco.

Going to Extremes

In completing the list of business tactics I wish every lawyer had in his repertoire, I would like to talk briefly about the dynamics of deals that turn out to be either real dogs or *too good*.

Realistically, the degree of success of deals can probably be mapped in keeping with the classic bell curve.

A small percentage turn out to be major windfalls.

Another small percentage are real disasters, ending in default, bankruptcy, and/or litigation.

The overwhelming majority end up somewhere in between. They are neither fantasies nor nightmares. They work about as well as you would expect them to work.

That fact notwithstanding, here's an axiom I would like lawyers and business people to pay heed to:

McCormack's Axiom of Wild Extremes

There are major psychological advantages in approaching a contract with the expectation that the deal in question will either be a *huge* success or a *monstrous* failure.

156

Both extremes present dangers, and both extremes offer opportunities.

Convince Me

Now, no one *really* goes into any deal expecting it to be a dismal flop.

Still, in almost any negotiation, there is a 'courting party' and a party being courted – and of course the party being courted has the leverage.

That leverage can be enhanced by the strategic use of pessimism.

The party being courted can say, in effect, 'I'm not convinced this deal is going to work, and if you want me, you've got to give me a great deal of reassurance. *I'm assuming the worst. Convince me otherwise.*'

This was a strategem we used in 1985 in representing Herschel Walker, when we negotiated an extension of his contract with the New Jersey Generals in the now-defunct United States Football League.

Clearly, Walker had the leverage in this negotiation. He was a known quantity – one of the best players in professional football and the USFL's number one drawing card. On the other hand, the USFL was still a fledgling enterprise and, as we all know, the history of pro sports is littered with leagues that never quite got off the ground.

So we took the stance that, for all we knew, the USFL might go belly-up tomorrow morning.

Starting from that point, we could argue that Walker should be paid a hefty premium for taking on that risk. We could also reasonably insist on getting General owner Donald Trump's *personal guarantee* of the running back's $6 million salary.

What makes this strategic pessimism such a powerful weapon **is that the courting party has no choice but to be optimistic.**

Trump was wooing Walker with rosy visions of the new league's future; he couldn't very well turn around and make it seem like he was lacking in faith.

To be consistent, Trump *had* to give Walker all due assurances. Our job was to make sure those assurances cost plenty.

Tanks for the Memories

In a sense, taking advantage of the newness of the USFL was almost too easy. Anyone with any brains realized that the new league would have to compensate in dollars for what it couldn't offer in security and prestige.

More impressive, then, is the situation where strategic pessimism is applied to deals that *don't* have obvious built-in dangers.

Consider this masterstroke pulled off a few years ago by my friend Bruce Rappaport.

Rappaport is a tremendously successful shipbuilder, maritime expert, banker, financier, oil man *and* lawyer – in short, one of the more brilliant businessmen in the world. He made legal history in his dealings with the Indonesian government and its state-owned oil company, Pertamina.

In striking an agreement with Pertamina to lease from it a number of tankers, Rappaport paid shrewd attention to what then seemed a highly unlikely worst-case scenario: what if the world oil picture radically changed, and those tankers could no longer be run at a profit?

This, you understand, was an eventuality that almost no one was considering back then, so Rappaport had little trouble getting the Indonesian government to co-sign and guarantee the contract.

Sure enough, the oil glut hit shortly thereafter, overcapacity in tankers became a tremendous problem in the shipping business – and almost everyone *except* Bruce Rappaport got badly hurt. He had been smart enough to anticipate disaster even during go-go times.

Too Good to Be True

Covering the downside is, of course, a vital part of every negotiation. Less obvious – and therefore more intriguing – is the need to guard against things going *too well*.

Human nature is funny. If you and I are fifty-fifty partners

158

in a deal, and together we make a dollar, you may think, 'Hey, that's pretty good – I made fifty cents.'

But if we make a *million* dollars, chances are you may say to yourself, 'Hey, why should that so-and-so McCormack be making five hundred thousand bucks off *me*?'

This leads me to posit this axiom:

McCormack's Axiom of Geometrical Greed

As the pie gets bigger, people start thinking less about their slice of it than about the *other* guy's.

This is obviously not a logical reaction, but I have seen it happen again and again. People get greedier in accordance with the gross amounts that are being divvied up, *even when their porportional split stays exactly the same.*

People tend not to think about this in the early stages of a deal, of course. They think they'll just get happier and happier, the more lucrative the arrangement turns out to be for all concerned.

For that reason, I am a firm believer in preparing *early* for the almost inevitable conflicts that set in when a deal turns out to be a windfall.

Some years ago IMG negotiated a contract with an Italian clothing manufacturer named Cerruti 1881 Sport, on behalf of our client Mats Wilander.

Wilander was just on the verge of breaking into the very top ranks of pro tennis, and he had the talent to stay near the top for some years. What this meant, among other things, was that the monies due him, in bonuses and royalties, would grow to impressive – but dangerous – amounts.

The clothing manufacturer, riding Wilander's growing celebrity, would be making money hand over fist; still, I could foresee that Cerruti would come to resent the outlays, and might well seek ways of getting out of the contract.

Accordingly, I urged our lawyers, *from the very outset*, to write in language protecting us, ironically, from the deal's possible runaway success.

I wanted a clause stipulating American jurisdiction in case of breach or default.

I wanted a provision allowing us to collect monies directly from United States department stores in the event of the manufacturer failing to pay us.

Some of these demands were met, some were not – and I had the feeling, frankly, that even my own lawyers thought I was being overly cautious and too much of a stickler on these points.

But sure enough, just as the royalties due to our client were reaching the psychological barrier of the million-dollar mark, the clothing manufacturer made an effort to terminate the contract. We were forced to sue, and eventually won.

I will close this chapter with a sobering lesson not dispensed in law school, but of potential value to every lawyer:

When a deal seems too good to be true, it usually is.

PART III

The Terrible Truth

8

Sometimes the System Doesn't Work

If you ever want to see a lawyer squirm, ask him the following simple question.

In what percentage of legal actions is justice ultimately done?

I myself have posed this query to a number of attorneys over the years – sometimes in a friendly way, sometimes less so – and I have never yet received a straightforward and satisfactory response.

Typically, a lawyer will answer by talking all around the subject.

He will tell you, for example, that there is no law school course or law school textbook titled *Justice*.

He will tell you that all of us have to live with the burdensome realization that life is unfair.

He will tell you that no code of laws is infallible, and that the most the laws can do is put a brake on people's natural cussedness.

Maybe he will commit himself as far as saying that justice is done more often than not – though frankly even that hazy claim to 51 per cent validity might not stand up to rigorous scrutiny.

To be fair, the question is impossible to answer; no one can pinpoint the proportion of just results.

Still, stating the issue in that way makes us realize that, in our hearts and in our consciences, we feel that **any answer less than 100 per cent is morally, if not practically, unacceptable.**

And it's also safe to say that the percentage of just results in legal actions is dramatically below one hundred.

This chapter is about some of the things that can go wrong in legal proceedings, *not* by chance, *not* necessarily because of malice, *but because the system is made that way.*

Insofar as it is possible to protect oneself from these systematic flaws, I will offer some advice on how to do so.

In situations where there doesn't seem to *be* any way to protect oneself, I will try to provide a map, at least, of what one can expect to encounter in the procedural trenches.

Legally speaking, the terrible truth is that it's a jungle out there.

The Strange Case of Dr Columbu

Let me tell you about the worst thing that has ever happened to our company in a court of law.

It's a sad tale, and in some respects it doesn't make a lot of sense. But I want to tell it in some detail because our general counsel, Bill Carpenter, maintains that the case provides a perfect shorthand example of much of what is cockeyed about the American tort, or personal injury, system.

Back in 1977, our television subsidiary, Trans World International, undertook to produce a show called *The World's Strongest Man.*

The format of the programme was a contest among various world-class bodybuilders, weightlifters, and so forth; and the show's 'hook' – the concept that would make the show irresistible to a broad audience – was that, rather than throwing barbells around, the participants would perform feats of strength that ordinary people could relate to and marvel at.

For instance, our ideas for events included lifting the front end of a car or pulling a tram loaded head high with cinder blocks.

The *pièce de résistance* of the programme was the so-called refrigerator race, in which contestants carried 400-pound refrigerators, in specially designed carriers, over a 40-yard course.

The idea, as filtered through the civil courts of the state of California, went on to cost us a million dollars.

Some background is in order. At the time *The World's Strongest Man* was conceived, we were well covered by liability insurance. Between the time we contracted to produce the show, however, and the time we actually taped it, our insurance was cancelled. The insurer, with the smug and unaccountable independence for which the insurance industry has become notorious, had simply and unilaterally decided not to cover us any more.

(This – for those keeping score – can be chalked up as point number one of why the tort system is in such miserable shape. **The insurance industry has been abdicating its proper role.** Insurance companies *should* help active, wealth-producing businesses function. These days, they tend simply to drain resources and to be so intent on protecting *themselves* that they don't really protect their clients.)

Anyway, the cancellation left us in a bind. We had agreed to indemnify both MCA, on whose lot the programme would be staged, and CBS, which would air the programme. We had already spent considerable sums launching the project and had already invited the contestants.

We *could* have reneged on our commitments, but doing so would have been costly and embarrassing, and might have damaged our credibility on future programmes.

So we decided to go ahead. Factored into this decision was our awareness that we were dealing with world-class athletes who understood and willingly accepted the risks of their profession, and *who had all signed a very clearly and carefully worded release.*

No one had ever been seriously injured at an IMG event, and we were confident that adequate precautions had been taken so that no one would be injured at this one.

But that was before Dr Franco Columbu, in the 1978 instalment of the show, decided to one-up his opponents by trying to *run* with a 400-pound refrigerator on his back.

No one *told* him to run, and in fact, according to at least some of the testimony at the eventual trial, he was advised *not* to run.

Nevertheless, he ran.

His knee became dislocated.

And suddenly we all embarked on a very different sort of contest.

I would like to make it clear that I bear no ill will at all towards Franco Columbu. In fact, I admire him. I have a genuine respect for the discipline that made him a great bodybuilder – possibly the second greatest ever, after his close friend Arnold Schwartzenegger. I respect the intelligence and foresight that led Columbu to become a chiropractor even while pursuing his athletic career. And needless to say, I sympathize with his injury. Who wouldn't?

But sympathy is an emotional concept, not a legal one.

This rudimentary distinction seems to have been utterly overlooked – as it so often is – in the course of his suit against us.

Giving the devil his due, Columbu's lawyer was very intelligent and had among his tools a number of intuitions of the sort one doesn't learn in law school, and that no attorney, client or business person can afford to be without.

So central are these intuitions, in fact, that they might be thought of as the Three Truths of the Plaintiff's Bar:

– Truth 1: Juries will almost always favour an individual over a corporation, especially if that corporation (like CBS and MCA, which were named as defendants even though *we* were the financially liable party) is perceived to have deep pockets.

– Truth 2: Less well-off jurors, perhaps savouring a plaintiff's windfall vicariously, are nearly always more inclined to award large sums than are jurors who are better off.

– Truth 3: Many, and perhaps most, judges, from the conscious or unconscious inclination 'to stick up for the little guy', will give more slack, procedurally speaking, to a plaintiff's lawyer than to a defendant's

With these truths in mind, let's look at some of the Columbu case's salient features.

Before the trial itself even started, the judge ruled, at the request of plaintiff's counsel, that Columbu's signed release *be excluded from evidence altogether*!

We simply wanted to include the release as evidence that Columbu, a professional athlete, had been made aware of the inherent risks and had accepted them. The judge disallowed this, purportedly out of a concern that *it might confuse the jury*.

In keeping with Truth 3, however, the judge didn't seem to worry about the jury being confused by the *plaintiff's* side.

Columbu's lawyer took the procedural liberty of asking Arnold Schwartzenegger, *by general knowledge the plaintiff's good friend*, to *speculate* about the economic losses suffered by Columbu on account of his injury.

According to the trial transcript, Schwartzenegger's testimony included admissions that the money to be made from bodybuilding 'is quite different from one person to the other', that 'you cannot hit it exactly on the mark', and that 'there is no way . . . [to] pinpoint it'.

In spite of that, Schwartzenegger went on to *estimate* — despite defence counsel's objections, which were overruled — that Columbu had lost more money as a result of his injury than he had ever made in his life; more money, actually, than any bodybuilder, except Schwartzenegger himself, had ever managed to earn from the sport and its resultant publicity.

Additionally, while the plaintiff had claimed that the design of the refrigerator carrier was faulty, the jury ended up acknowledging that it was *not*. In fact, a case could be made that the mechanism had saved Columbu's life because when his leg buckled, the carrier device did its job and suspended him in mid-air rather than letting him fall to the ground with the refrigerator on top of him.

Shortly after the accident, Columbu had acknowledged to commentator Brent Musberger that the mishap was his own fault and he should not have tried to run.

For all that, in keeping with Truth 1, the jury's sympathies were with *the individual who admitted he had made a mistake, rather than with the corporation that had been shown not to be negligent.*

And the judgment? Well, that fell in squarely with Truth 2.

What sort of damages would you expect to have been awarded? Fifty thousand dollars? A hundred thousand dollars? Well, it was $1,036,760 – and you'll forgive me for saying I believe the jurors probably took more vicarious satisfaction from Columbu's payday than was seemly.

One more detail: by the time the trial took place, in 1982, *Columbu had made such a complete recovery that he had won the 1981 Mr Olympia contest.*

Sworn witnesses had also seen him lifting up cars in the Los Angeles area.

The jury knew all that. It didn't seem to matter to them.

As a postscript to this odd tale, I should mention that we filed an appeal. Two hundred thousand dollars in legal fees brought us *halfway* through the appeals process, at which point we settled for $800,000. The total made a nice round number.

You Think You Got Troubles?

A million dollars for a temporarily hurt knee is a pretty high ticket. But we don't kid ourselves that we were anywhere near the pinnacle of absurdity, so far as liability handouts are concerned. Consider these recent awards:

– In 1984 a California woman, who was driving her husband's Porsche after having had several drinks, had an accident in which her passenger was killed. She had been doing 60 m.p.h. in a 25 m.p.h. zone. Porsche was ordered to pay $2.5 million for having designed a car deemed too high-performance for the average driver.

– In 1985 an overweight man with a heart condition bought a lawnmower from Sears. He later had a heart attack while starting the mower and was awarded $1.8 million.

168

– While in the process of attempting to burgle a school, a man fell through a skylight. The company that insured the school was ordered to pay $260,000 in damages and to give the would-be burglar $1500 a month for life.

– In Maryland two men tried to dry their hot-air balloon in a commercial-laundry dryer. The dryer exploded, injuring them slightly, and they ended up winning almost $900,000 in damages.

– Back in sunny California, a man was injured when a drunk driver rammed into the phone booth in which he was making a call. The state's chief justice ruled that the company that designed the phone booth was liable for the man's injuries.

The Law as Lottery

Odd stories like the above, by their sheer illogicality and craziness, make headlines and may even elicit grim smiles from many of us.

But they suggest a situation that is not funny in the least.

The terrible truth is that the American tort system is raging out of control, operating less like a cogent mechanism for redressing wrongs than like a lottery in which 'lucky victims' find themselves with windfall profits.

The problem, of course, is that those windfalls come at *our* expense. Juries tend to give away corporations' money as if it came from thin air. In fact, it comes from consumers like us.

How does this dynamic work?

Consider the ripple effects of a case like Columbu's.

Having been badly stung on the Columbu lawsuit, we have to be that much more intent on covering ourselves next time around. Either we buy coverage *at whatever price an insurer will deign to sell it to us*, or we 'go bare' – that is, proceed without insurance – in which case we need to keep a reserve fund against possible disaster.

Either way, our operating costs have been jacked up.

Maybe we can swallow some of the increase; we can't

169

swallow all of it. So we go to the network – ABC, say – for which we're preparing the programme, and we tell them that we need to charge a little more than we did the last time.

ABC, being realistic and well aware of the judicial and insurance climate, is sympathetic and agrees to the higher price.

The network, in turn, goes to the show's sponsor – Ford Motor Company, let's say – and tells them that, since the network is paying more for the programming, commercial time is going to cost a little more, too.

What is Ford going to do – stop advertising on television? Obviously not. Ford understands the fiscal pressures behind the increased cost, and passes that increase right along to the consumer in the prices of its cars.

Taking the ripple effects one step further, for a certain number of consumers that increased price will be the last straw that convinces them to keep their old car for a few more years, and there go a few more jobs.

If jurors thought a little more about this whole chain of events, they might realize that their 'generous' awards aren't really very generous.

The Real Villains

But jurors come and jurors go, and it doesn't make much sense to blame *them* for the basic flaws in the legal system.

On the contrary, the basic flaws were put in by the people who *made* the legal system – i.e., the lawyers.

And since lawyers made the system by which they make their living, it shouldn't come as much of a surprise that **most of the most profound flaws in Western jurisprudence have to do with giving lawyers too much power and control.**

This excessive and misplaced power exists at several levels.

Obviously, it pertains at the level of *individual* cases, as we will shortly illustrate.

But it *also* applies at the *political* level – the level at which reforms can be made, or squelched.

There is no great mystery about what can and should be done to help bring our liability system into line with sanity and fiscal responsibility:

1. A cap should be placed on jury awards for physical harms, and such hazy concepts as 'pain and suffering' should either be more clearly defined or be got rid of.

2. Contingent fees should operate on a sliding scale – for example, 25 per cent on the first $100,000, 10 per cent thereafter – to remove some of the incentive for the 'moonshot mentality'.

To their shame, the men and women of the plaintiff's bar have consistently lobbied against these reforms.

So intent are they on preserving their turf that they have managed to subvert even the one reform that *has* been legislated: no-fault car insurance – which has turned out not to be no-fault at all!

And just in case there is anybody out there who harbours illusions about the general moral tone prevailing among the plaintiff's bar, let me report on the results of an interesting experiment conducted recently by *The American Lawyer* magazine.

The publication sent one of its reporters, posing as an accident victim, to thirteen attorneys. She told each one that she had taken a fall *near* a construction site, *but that the fall was in no way caused by or connected to the construction*.

Five of the thirteen lawyers advised her to **change her recollection of the mishap to bring it closer to the site so they could sue!**

The Servant as Master

Akio Morita, the founder and chairman of Sony, is one of many non-Westerners who have been shocked by the arrogance and pushiness of American attorneys, and in his recent autobiography Morita tells a story that illustrates perfectly what can happen when lawyers are too much in control in specific cases.

171

Way back in 1968, an American trade group called the Electronic Industries Association filed a complaint with the US Treasury Department, accusing Japanese firms of 'dumping' television sets – that is, selling them below cost in order to destroy competition – on the US market.

This was a long, bitter and complicated suit, and Sony was eventually omitted from the list of firms under investigation for a very simple reason: *as purveyor of one of the highest-priced brands on the market, Sony couldn't very logically be accused of unfair low-balling*!

That, however, didn't stop an American television maker, National Union Electric Company (whose brand name was Emerson), from filing a *private* suit against Sony. Notwithstanding the Treasury Department findings, NUE pressed its suit with such thoroughness that it dragged on for twelve and a half years.

Now, Akio Morita is a practical man. He is not easily angered, nor does he stand on ceremony.

He was confident that Sony would 'win' the suit – which eventually it did. But he also understood that the 'victory' would be meaningless.

The lawsuit was *an unproductive sort of competition*.

It improved neither company's products. It benefited neither company's employees or shareholders.

By draining energy and funds, it weakened *both* companies vis-à-vis the open marketplace.

So Morita paid a personal call on Hans Werthen, the chairman of Electrolux, which in turn owned NUE. Morita politely explained why he felt the lawsuit should be laid to rest.

Werthen told him that he might be interested in settling, *but that he couldn't commit to it because he was afraid his own lawyers might sue him*!

NUE's attorneys, you see, were working on a contingency basis, and the suit asked for damages in the amount of $360 million. If the suit were dropped on orders from Electrolux, the lawyers could, in theory, sue for the money they *might* have made *if* they had won the original battle.

In other words, the chairman of the board was powerless to call off his own attorneys. The servants had become the master.

Morita was floored by this turn of events, which could never have happened in Japan.

The terrible truth is that once a certain threshold of complexity and expense has been crossed, there is a real danger in business life that attorneys will take over decisions that *should* be left to executives.

Tennis Schizophrenia

Let me give another example, closer to home, of this dynamic in action.

At this writing, IMG is involved in a tremendously complicated antitrust suit, the subject of which is nothing short of who does and can do what in the sport of professional tennis.

Since this suit is still pending, I cannot talk about it in much detail. However, the point I want to make has to do with the schizophrenia that sets in when lawyers do battle while business people are still doing business.

There are no fewer than *nine* entities seriously interested in this anti-trust suit, and even as the legal war heats up, we are actively doing business on an ongoing basis with *seven* of them! These entities include several national and international tennis federations, players' associations, and so forth, and lawsuit or no lawsuit, none of us can afford *not* to keep doing business with each other!

It would seem to be in everybody's best interest to be cooperative and flexible in working out their differences. But because there is a lawsuit, the lawyers are running the show instead. One of the principals involved has *publicly* announced that since he has insurance that picks up all legal costs, why should he even *think* of settling?

He (and his lawyers) have a meal ticket for as long as the suit drags on, while most of the principals, I would guess, have reached the juncture where they would just as soon negotiate and get on with their lives.

If only the lawyers would let them.

Are there ways to avoid losing control in legal matters?

The answer is yes and no.

Since the system itself is skewed towards the lawyers' advantage, there will always be situations in which snowballing complexity and ever-higher stakes will pull matters out of the principals' control.

J. Paul Getty had lawsuits he couldn't settle. Howard Hughes placed himself in situations where legal processes could not be stopped. No one is rich enough or powerful enough to control the machinery once a certain momentum has been established.

However, one can stay in control *most* of the time **by taking firm and decisive steps before the momentum has reached that threshold:**

1. Make it clear to your attorney early on – preferably in writing – that you intend to retain *sole and final discretion* as to when and whether the matter should be settled.

   If the attorney protests that this undercuts his chances of a fat contingent fee, either negotiate a provision whereby *a flat or hourly rate* will be paid in case of settlement – or get a different lawyer.

2. Do a calm and sober cost-benefit analysis to determine at which point(s) it might make sense for you to bail out. Remember: *in almost every instance, the longer a suit drags on, the higher the proportion of benefits accruing to the lawyers!*

   In real terms, settling for fifty cents on the dollar *early in the game* is very often a better deal than a higher figure down the road.

3. Always be sceptical when a lawyer tells you you're going to win, and *keep in mind the following axiom*:

174

> **McCormack's Axiom of Stubborn Hope**
>
> There is nothing likelier than excessive optimism to pull you into a runaway suit that never ends!

THE CLIENT AS VILLAIN

In the preceding examples, the principals in legal actions have been portrayed as reasonable and rational, and it's the lawyers themselves who have been shown to be manipulative and self-aggrandizing.

But, of course, that's not always how it works.

In the typical instance, the lawyer just does the client's bidding – and *if the proceedings get nasty, it may be because the client's purpose is nasty to begin with.*

They don't teach it this way at law school, but the terrible truth is that **the law is a game** – full of paradoxes and of opportunities that exist on the fringe of fair play.

The same system, for example, that piously asserts that contracts are sacred offers myriad ways of breaking con tracts.

And a big part of what clients ask their lawyers to do is to seek out the glitches and the loopholes: **to use the letter of the law to subvert the spirit of the law.**

That this can be done certainly constitutes a big flaw in our system. But then I have never heard of any system that can't be turned against itself somehow.

For practical purposes, the idea is **to understand how those twists and turns can be employed against you, and to deal with them as they occur.**

A KILLING ON KILLY

Consider the case in which Jean-Claude Killy was essentially *forced* to become a plaintiff against the giant conglomerate

AMF, and in which he had to squander a considerable portion of his wealth in the process of claiming what was rightfully his.

Killy was one of our earliest clients. He was also, in the years following his unprecedented three gold medals in alpine skiing in the 1968 Olympics at Grenoble, one of the most sought-after personalities in sport.

Killy was handsome, he was charming, and he was undisputed champion of a pastime that was becoming synonymous with cosmopolitan glamour and sophistication. The ski industry was absolutely booming in those years, and its demographics were a dream.

Those were also the years when wooden skis were giving place to plastic and fibreglass, and the Head Ski Company found itself lagging behind some of its more adventurous competitors in the transition. It was becoming clear that fibreglass skis were the wave of the future, and Head needed to make up for lost time by entering that field with a lot of visibility.

What better way to do it than with skis autographed by Jean-Claude Killy?

We negotiated a contract which provided that Killy would get certain minimum guarantees against a royalty on sales of all non-wooden skis.

What happened, of course, was that from year to year, a higher and higher percentage of skis were non-wooden, and Killy's earnings moved up accordingly. Head soon became a leader in the high-tech ski business, Killy was making several hundred thousand dollars a year from his endorsement, and everybody was happy.

Then Head was bought out by AMF.

It took the new regime about a year to go through its existing contracts. When they finally did so, AMF apparently decided that Killy was costing them too much money.

The company itself was doing fabulously well, but, as so often happens, the new management came to resent the deal made by the old; they wanted to build monuments of their own, not be burdened with those of the old regime.

Besides, their fibreglass ski business was well established by now, and AMF could reach the smug conclusion that it simply didn't need Killy any more.

AMF's tactics for getting out of its contract were simple, cynical and eventually effective: it would just stop paying Killy, force him to sue, defend these actions on whatever grounds came to hand, and simply wear down the skier in terms of time, trouble and expense.

Killy had no option except to fall in with the script.

He sued. To do so, he had to hire American lawyers, and pay them out of pocket. He also had to fly himself and his representatives back and forth from Switzerland, where he lived, to the United States for an endless series of depositions.

With the expected trial still a year or two away, the skier had shelled out around $350,000 in fees and expenses. Additionally, he had been subjected to various annoyances, embarrassments and invasions of privacy.

AMF, ironically enough, had decided to defend its unconscionable reneging on *moral* grounds. It claimed that Killy was leading a life of decadence that was reflecting badly on the products of the Head Ski Company.

Could anything be more ridiculous?

Sponsors had originally flocked to Killy precisely because his image of the carefree bachelor — an image exaggerated and to some degree *created* by the media and the sponsors themselves — was part of their scheme for selling the 'skiing life style' (or fantasy thereof).

Now AMF was trying to free itself of a corporate expense on the grounds that Killy liked champagne and was living with a woman to whom he was not married (but later did marry).

But the sad truth is that one doesn't have to be reasonable to get what one wants out of a lawsuit.

AMF, after all, could afford its lawyers a lot more easily than Killy could afford *his*.

Additionally, the corporation had the home-court advantage of US jurisdiction.

And it had the commercial benefit of Killy's name on a huge inventory of skis even as it was giving Killy a hard time.

177

If all that sounds unfair, it was. And it suggests a central paradox about the law as it is actually practised: while the scales of justice, in theory, start off level, much of what passes for 'legal expertise' consists of cleverness in tipping them – by whatever means. **When there's money on the table, most people lose their gusto for a fair fight.**

Eventually, Killy had to settle for a fixed-fee payment from AMF and a termination of his arrangement with Head. He was clearly in the right, but he had no choice but to give up.

The fight had simply become too expensive – as AMF knew it would.

This was not law as justice, but law as a battle of attrition.

The Problem of Injustice

Stories like the above, I realize only too well, leave a bad taste.

Unfairness rankles.

The feeling of helplessness breeds rage.

How, then, should people deal with injustice – not just in practical terms, but *emotionally*?

How do you handle it when you know, to put it bluntly, that you have been screwed?

Clearly, this is a highly individual question, and people deal with it in various ways, from getting ulcers to having a couple more martinis.

Here's how I deal with it:

1. I remind myself that legal battles are almost always schematic – that is, player A against player B, with little or nothing *personal* involved.

Remembering this doesn't help with the *practical* loss, but it eases the anger by making me realize it wasn't the *flesh-and-blood me* that was under attack.

2. I tell myself that while a result may be unjust in any given case, the total of *all* results will probably even out. As in other games, with law you win some and you lose some.

3. I comfort myself with the patient hope that I may have a chance to get even somewhere down the road.

The *first* legal system, after all, was 'an eye for an eye and a tooth for a tooth' – and don't ever let anyone tell you that people don't look forward to revenge.

9

A Few Good Reasons
Not to Sue

Yes, revenge can be sweet.

Furthermore, seeking revenge *through the courts* has become so much a part of our national customs that we sue each other almost by reflex.

We sue each other so often, and *with such unquestioning assurance that that's how things are done*, that some legal scholars have dubbed it 'the litigious society'.

The litigious society is based on a few assumptions which we take so much for granted that it hardly occurs to us to question them.

We assume that whenever someone suffers an injury or a loss, there's a *someone else* who's responsible.

This assumption has two corollaries:

It seeks to do away with the concept of plain bad luck.

It suggests that if ten thousand people step around a hole in the sidewalk and *you* fall in, you're not a klutz for doing so; it's someone else's fault.

We assume that every wrong has a remedy, and that the remedy can be provided by human mandate.

This obviously is not the way it happened during most of human history. When God caused Job's crops to fail, Job did not seek damages. When the barbarians sacked Rome, the Romans did not expect to have their losses made good.

We assume that *going to court* is the best if not the only way to seek redress.

Like bickering siblings, we look to the court as to an all-wise parent, too often losing sight of the fact that the court is subject to the same prejudices, lapses in judgement, and blind spots as we are.

The Downside

Those are our assumptions. We cling to them so fervently that we tend to overlook all the things that are *wrong* with litigation:

1. It costs too much.
2. It takes too long.
3. It benefits the lawyers too much and the clients too little.
4. It opens the gates to a flood of complications that take time and energy away from productive pursuits.

The Costs

Much has already been said in these pages about the steep and, in some cases, unconscionable charges that are rung up in connection with legal matters. For the present, however, I would just like to mention the concept of *threshold amounts*.

Pursuing litigation is so expensive that most companies have a policy, stated or otherwise, of not bothering to sue for amounts under the threshold of *half a million dollars*.

That seems to be about the point at which the benefits start to outweigh the costs. Since corporations routinely sue each other for much more than that amount, the threshold is reasonable.

But what about individuals?

Typically, suits between individuals are for smaller amounts. But a funny thing happens to fees and expenses in lawsuits: they always go up when the stakes get higher, but they hardly ever come down when the stakes are lower.

In other words, *the smaller the suit, the higher the proportion of expenses.*

And the higher the proportion of expenses, the smaller the chance of coming out *meaningfully* ahead.

The Law's Delay

If the expense were the only drawback, I would say go ahead and buy your day in court; you'll feel better for it.

No one, however, feels good about the law's delay.

According to no less an authority than William Shakespeare, the slowness of legal procedures – the wall of molasses – is one of the 'slings and arrows' that might well drive a man to despair or even suicide.

In Hamlet's famous 'To be, or not to be' soliloquy, 'the law's delay' ranks right up there with 'the oppressor's wrong' and 'the pangs of dispriz'd love' among the irritations 'that make calamity of so long life'.

There are times when *any* result, even a bad result, gets to seem preferable to the endless waiting, the endless review, the endless string of correspondence, of appearances, of hopes raised and hopes dashed.

The Why of It

Why do legal matters, and especially litigation, take so long?

Ironically, many and perhaps most legal delays have to do with the so-called 'protections' built into the system.

At law school, students are taught that these 'protections' allow both sides fair access to information and pertinent sources, due process for appeal, and so forth.

Like so many well-intentioned elements of our laws, however, the 'protections' usually backfire.

They don't protect anybody – or at least not the people who *should* be protected.

In effect, what the 'protections' do is **to set up an elaborate game in which stalling tactics figure prominently and in which, since time is money, the side with the bigger war chest has a definite edge,** irrespective of the merits of the case.

Although it's not a phrase that people learn in law school, and it's not a strategy that the American Bar Association

182

officially endorses, the tactic of choice in many cases is simply 'to spend the other side to death'.

This lends fresh meaning to the old cliché about 'buying time'.

The Fortune 500 v. Me

Let me tell you a strange and rather complicated story that persuasively illustrates the law's delay in action – or, I should say, inaction.

This story begins in 1974 – when Gerald Ford was president and 'China' still meant Taiwan – and, as of this writing, the case is yet to be resolved.

Dollar one has yet to change hands – except of course between clients and attorneys, where many, many dollars have new owners.

Back in 1974 I made an agreement with Russ Meyer, who was then the chief executive officer of Grumman Aircraft Corporation. Meyer and I had known each other for years – ever since we worked together at Arter, Hadden. Meyer is a unique and versatile man who eventually left Arter, Hadden, to become CEO of American Aviation, subsequently acquired by Grumman.

Now, in 1974 Russ and I had a talk about Grumman's efforts to sell private or corporate jets to very wealthy individuals. At this level of the market, the great difficulty was entrée. How did you get the ear of the decision maker? How did you arrange for an appropriate introduction that might lead to a sale?

As it happened, I knew someone who I thought might be interested in buying a jet, and mentioned this to Russ. Russ asked where this individual lived, and when I answered Europe, Russ confidently told me that Grumman already knew of every prospective buyer on the Continent.

I then proposed an arrangement: I would tell Russ the name of the man I had in mind. If he was already listed in Grumman's files, then that would be the end of it.

If he wasn't known to Grumman, I would set up an introduction, and in the event that the introduction led to a sale, I would receive a finder's fee. We agreed that reasonable value for my services would be $50,000, based on an anticipated purchase price of $3.75 million for the plane.

Sure enough, the prospective buyer was not listed in Grumman's files; and off we went to Switzerland to meet the gentleman in question.

This, to repeat, was 1974. Nothing at all happened till 1978; then two things occurred almost simultaneously.

The man to whom I had introduced the Grumman executives finally went ahead and bought a plane – not for $3.75 million, as had been projected four years earlier, but for $7.5 million. That was the good news.

The bad news was that Russ Meyer left Grumman to become chairman and CEO of Cessna.

Russ Meyer's personal behaviour throughout had been totally honourable, as I hope is clear. He told me of his impending move, and informed me that, as part of his wrapping-up process at the company, he had reminded his number two man, *both verbally and in a written memo*, of the valid commitment that the company had had to me since 1974, and still had.

Nevertheless, when the sale of the aircraft was completed, and I informed Grumman's new management of the money they owed me, they reneged.

I had no choice but to sue for $100,000 – keeping my commission in proportion to the price of the aircraft.

Thus began an adventure in the courts of the state of New York that has featured both high drama and low comedy, that has resulted in lawyers on both sides being reprimanded by the bar association, and that has been a *veritable source-book on the stalling tactics that can be used by a company with virtually limitless resources and with plenty of in-house counsel looking for things to do.*

ROUND 1
Grumman's first ploy was to try to have the case thrown out by way of a 'summary judgment'.

The company claimed, in brief, that there had never been a real agreement between Grumman and me, and that Russ Meyer had given me a 'sweetheart deal' on his departure from the corporation.

In other words, the 1974 conversation had never taken place, and Meyer and I were supposedly in collusion to rip off Grumman.

This allegation, aside from being ludicrous, was insulting to both Russ Meyer and me, and ironically, in a context other than a court of law, might very well have constituted slander.

The motion for summary judgment was denied – since Grumman's own internal memoranda recorded the existence of the deal!

In any event, this opening gambit took six months.

ROUND 2
It also set the down-and-dirty, no-holds-barred tone for much of what was to follow.

Still, it didn't suggest the rather bizarre confrontation that would occur during the *second* drawn-out phase of the case – the taking of depositions.

Having lost its attempt at disclaiming the deal outright, Grumman now changed tactics and decided it would base its argument on the contention that the aeroplane had been sold *not* to the person whom I had introduced to the company, but to his *unincorporated business*.

Technically, this was true – but meaningless.

How many people buy a $7.5 million aeroplane and *don't* put the transaction in the name of a business?

The point was that *this buyer had made the purchase decision*, and, further, that *the plane was mainly for his own use*.

Grumman denied this altogether and claimed, in fact, that it had had *no direct contact whatsoever* with the individual involved.

There is a phase in a lawsuit known as 'discovery'. In principle, discovery is intended to let each side solicit pertinent documents and records from the other so that, in theory, the case can be argued from the fullest possible complement of facts.

Discovery tends to be an unspeakably tedious chore (see, for example, *Geffine v. Doyle*!), and can itself be used as a stalling device. But it can also be a powerful weapon for an attorney who is diligent at doing it.

As it happened, my attorney did it *very* diligently. *So* diligently, in fact, that at a pretrial deposition during which Grumman's attorney was maintaining the no-personal-contact stance, my lawyer produced a memo *from Grumman's files* – obtained through normal discovery procedures – in which the person I'd introduced made it very clear, above his own signature, that he bought the plane, he used the plane, and in fact he had complaints about the performance of the plane!

To put it mildly, it did not make Grumman's lawyer look good to be informed of the existence of this document by the other side.

And when my attorney began – as was perfectly proper – to read the letter into the record, the other lawyer became totally flustered. He shouted, he protested; he said, groundlessly, that he would not allow the letter to be read.

The two attorneys were sitting side by side, and my lawyer finally had no choice but to turn his back on his blustering colleague so that the court reporter could hear his recital of the letter.

Grumman's lawyer seems to have panicked at this point, and he actually reached over my attorney's shoulder, presumably trying to snatch away the document! In doing so, he – we presume inadvertently – hit my attorney on the side of the head and jostled loose his glasses.

Now, my lawyer is about five feet five, and past the age of sixty. He is an urbane, charming, and non-violent man. However, he had been on his college boxing squad many years before, and some reflexes stay with you always. If you are hit, you hit back. Which is what he did.

Fortunately, there was a witness present who was thirty

years younger and a head taller than either of the battling elders, and he separated them before anyone was hurt.

The upshot was that both attorneys had to answer to the bar association for that incident – and Grumman's *second* attempt at a defence had been discredited.

ROUND 3

No matter. By the time the trial – the *first* trial – rolled around, the resourceful attorneys for the defence had another tack to try.

They now acknowledged that the man in question had in fact bought the plane, and they acknowledged that Russ Meyer had in fact written a memo confirming our agreement.

They claimed, however, that Meyer's memo was a legal nullity, as he had written it after the board had accepted his resignation.

Forget that the memo merely *reconfirmed* a deal that had been made years earlier. Grumman now maintained that Meyer, at the time he actually wrote the memo, did not have the authority legally to commit Grumman to anything.

To our surprise, Grumman won this round.

ROUND 4

But we appealed against this ruling, and won a reversal from a panel of five judges who better understood the business realities of Meyer's postresignation position.

As was clear at the trial, Meyer had been given *explicit, written instruction by Grumman's board to leave memoranda on all pending matters.*

Having been issued those instructions, he was still functioning as a bona fide officer of the company during the time of the sale; *ergo*, the memo was back to being binding.

Now *we'd* won.

This, by the way, brings us to 1983 – five years after the initial action!

187

ROUND 5

However, the panel that heard our appeal was empowered only to decide the matter in principle; the judges were not authorized to assess a judgment.

So now we had to go back for a *second* trial.

And guess what?

Grumman pulled *yet another* gambit out of its apparently bottomless bag of defences.

Simple common sense would tell you that if someone needs to try out five different arguments, he is probably grasping at straws; if an argument has merit, you need only one.

Part of the reason for the law's delay, then, is that lawyers are allowed to concoct a different story for every stage of a battle.

As ridiculous as one ploy is, you can wipe the slate clean and try another; *there's no real penalty* for trying people's credulity or patience, or even for proposing *mutually contradictory defences at various stages.*

This time, Grumman argued that it hadn't really sold a plane to the fellow I had introduced, *nor* to his corporation!

Rather, the company had sold a plane to the Italian film producer Dino de Laurentiis – and if you're surprised to have a new character introduced at this point in the tale, imagine how *we* felt.

The story was that de Laurentiis had ordered the plane, then, for some reason had decided not to take delivery.

Grumman, now acting *not* as an aeroplane manufacturer, but only as an agent for the film producer, arranged the transfer of that very plane to my contact.

Thus, the sale was between my client and the movie mogul; Grumman, which received only a $200,000 commission on the sale, contended that my fee – twelve years later – should be around 1½ per cent of *that*!

ROUND 6

However, if Grumman was arguing that the amount the commission would be based on should be *reduced*, I found I had grounds to claim it should be radically *increased*. My contact had bought two more aeroplanes from Grumman, bringing the total amount of his business with the company to around *$22 million.*

Why shouldn't my finder's fee be reckoned on the basis of the whole ledger?

ROUND 7 . . . AND COUNTING

So where has all this argumentation and legal ingenuity taken us?

Well, Grumman's main contention that it was only an 'agent' was discredited by the existence of a slightly embarrassing bill of sale between the company and the man I had introduced.

My contention that I should now receive a commission on the sale of all three aircraft was disallowed because Russ Meyer's memo was worded in such a way as to stipulate 'the sale of *an* aeroplane'.

The bottom line is that *I have yet to see a single cent from a claim that began in 1978.*

I was awarded an amount which, counting interest, was within a few thousand dollars of what I asked for to begin with.

Did that get me any money? Well, not quite.

Grumman made *another* appeal, still claiming it didn't really *sell* the plane and arguing that the record of the sale was just a book-keeping convenience. To keep things symmetrical, I *also* appealed, taking a shot at an increase in the amount of the award.

And what do you suppose? The appellate court *did* increase the amount! Perhaps there was one appeal too many.

But, there are still appellate courts left in the procedure that Grumman hasn't used yet.

Check with me in the year 2000.

The Common Thread

In all the ingenious tactics the lawyers employed in dragging out the Grumman case, a common theme exists: **they all use the law to defeat the law.**

189

And every client, in deciding whether a given matter is worth pursuing, should be aware that **any skilled lawyer can use these techniques to prolong a case almost indefinitely.**

The terrible truth is that **the longer a case goes on, the less it is worth, except to the lawyers.**

By now Grumman has certainly paid more in fees than it would have cost to give me what I had coming.

This is inexplicable except in terms of *the unproductive stubbornness and obsessiveness that lawsuits tend to breed.*

The Electronic Cottage Gone Berserk

Before leaving this subject of legal stalling, I would just like to mention one recent practical development that ironically was *intended* to make all of us more efficient, but which, in practice, has made it *unprecedentedly easy to become strangled in red tape.*

I'm talking about electronic word-processing.

Not long ago I heard a story about a businessman who made some stupid moves, and found himself with a half million dollars of personally guaranteed debt that he could not afford to pay.

He went to an attorney who was extremely clever but who had a limited conscience, and described his problem. The lawyer said to him: 'Give me five thousand dollars up front, and I will lay such a burden of discovery on these people that you won't have to shell out another penny for at least five years.'

There was no mention of right or wrong, guilt or innocence.

The soul and essence of the transaction was that five thousand dollars would buy five years.

How was this attorney able to offer such a bargain?

Simply by cranking up his word-processor, hitting a few buttons, and demanding that the other side hand over *thousands* of documents – letters, memos, invoices – that *might possibly* have some bearing on the case.

These demands are legal, according to the rules of discovery. The problem is that *demanding* documents and records has become diabolically easy, while *producing* these documents and records has remained as tedious and time-consuming as ever.

The papers still have to be scanned by human eyes.

Their significance still has to be appraised by human judgement.

Depending on the nature of the case, it can take a hundred or a thousand or ten thousand times as long to *furnish* documents as to demand that they be furnished.

The kicker is that **there is no way to know in advance what sort of research burdens will pertain in a given case.**

The lawyers' discretion is just too broad to be able to predict it.

This is one more good reason to consider letting the other side win by default sometimes.

The Pandora Syndrome

So much for the question of time.

Now let's look at the issue of control of one's own destiny.

In theory, people sue to stay in control, or to regain control, of their lives: **to assert the fact that they won't be pushed around.**

In actuality, however, **lawsuits tend to make one vulnerable to so many complications that they usually reduce the amount of control one has and make it *easier* to be pushed around.**

This happens because of a phenomenon that can be described in terms of another axiom:

McCormack's Pandora Axiom

Once you open the lid on conflicts and complications, those conflicts and complications generally multiply.

You find yourself in violation of clauses you never knew existed.

You find yourself confronted by regulations you never realized might pertain.

You find yourself fighting phantom opponents who weren't even part of the original disagreement!

And you come to realize that **normal business life is possible only because, most of the time, people ignore the kind of technicalities and nitpicking that nobody ignores once the lawyers have been brought in.**

Laver v. *Connors* v. *FCC* v. *Everybody*

Let me give you an example of the Pandora Syndrome at its most bedevilling.

Back in 1974, we conceived a tennis programme that became known as the CBS Heavyweight Championship of Tennis. Our idea, essentially, was to do away with the early rounds of a regular tournament, and just arrange a 'finals' between two top pros. Each player was to be paid a substantial guarantee, with an additional purse going to the winner.

The first match was played in 1975, at Caesar's Palace in Las Vegas, and pitted Rod Laver, who was managed by us, against Jimmy Connors, who was represented by a man named Bill Riordan.

Riordan and IMG co-promoted the match pursuant to a written agreement between us, and IMG's Barry Frank sold the television rights to CBS.

The match was a financial and artistic success. Connors won, so he would be a part of the following year's event.

That night, as Barry was leaving Caesar's Palace, he ran into Riordan in the casino. Barry congratulated Riordan on his client's win – and also congratulated Connors himself.

Barry suggested that next year's instalment should match Connors against John Newcombe; Riordan agreed that that would be a good idea.

Barry then remarked that IMG was close to Newcombe, who at the time was not a client, and would bring him in, in exchange for continuing the existing fifty/fifty co-promotion deal.

Riordan agreed and the two men shook hands.

Now, **that conversation constituted a contract.**

Among lay people, the concept of a verbal agreement seems to cause a fair amount of confusion. In fact, the definition is very precise. A verbal contract, like any contract, consists of:

1. an offer made;
2. that offer accepted; and
3. agreement as to a consideration, monetary or otherwise, to pass between the parties.

What happened, however, is that Bill Riordan, upon reflection, decided he didn't need us to get Newcombe or to handle television.

He cut us out of the deal, and we sued him.

We had Barry Frank, Barry Frank's wife and Jimmy Connors himself as witnesses to a conversation that Riordan was now claiming had never taken place.

So up to this point, what we're talking about has been a straightforward, two-party dispute.

But now, skipping ahead three years, the Pandora Syndrome kicks in.

Connors beat Newcombe in Heavyweight Championship match number two, and beat Guillermo Vilas in match number three. Match number four, against Manuel Orantes, was set up.

The suit between us and Riordan had become public knowledge, and it had a fair degree of gossip value among the press. So, for better or worse, the media were paying more attention to the Heavyweight series than they might otherwise have done.

By coincidence, Barry Frank at this time left our company and went to work as head of CBS Sports.

By coincidence again, Barry was sitting in a hotel room watching this *fourth* Heavyweight instalment between Connors and Orantes when he heard commentator Pat Summerall describe the match as a 'winner-take-all' event.

Well, Barry Frank knew damn well it wasn't a winner-take-all event.

It had started as a guarantee-plus-purse arrangement, and, in fact, the format had been changed from the original so that

193

it was now a winner-take-*nothing* event. Both players got guarantees, and that was it.

So Barry – who'd had nothing to do with contracting for this match – dutifully got on the phone, managed to get hooked up with the remote unit that was stationed at the event, and told the on-site people that they'd got their information very wrong and they'd been misrepresenting the event.

Now, here's Pandora at work: word of Barry's call to the TV truck soon became fairly common knowledge (Pat Summerall was particularly upset that he had been duped) and eventually leaked to the press.

And a reporter from the New York Times *went on to tell the whole world that CBS was lying about the match being winner-take-all.*

This led to an FCC complaint, which led, in turn, to considerable acrimony between CBS and Bill Riordan, who'd been producing events for as long as Connors had kept winning. Had Riordan been lying to the network about the format or had the network itself got its information wrong?

Now, since we were involved in a fight with Riordan, you might think we were pleased that Pandora was making his life miserable.

But not so fast . . .

The FCC, once it opened its investigation, looked very closely at *all* the programmes in the series, including the first one, which *we'd* produced.

And they found that, in the first instalment, Caesar's Palace had been given about fifty-seven plugs, both audio and video, and *there'd been no concluding acknowledgment that the casino had paid a promotional fee for the exposure.* (You know that standard line: 'A promotional fee has been paid by . . .'.)

So the FCC told CBS that the network was in violation of Section 317 of the Federal Communications Code, which requires that all such promotional arrangements be revealed on the air – and now CBS was mad at *us*. To make matters even worse, the FCC was, at that time, reviewing the renewal of the licence of KCBS, CBS's station in Los Angeles, which was valued at $300,000,000!

To cover themselves, the people from the network claimed they'd never been *told* that Caesar's Palace was paying a promotional fee – which meant that *we*, as producers, were in violation of Section 508, which stipulates that the providers of programming must inform the broadcaster of all promotional deals.

We claimed – and could document – that we *had* informed CBS of the Caesar's deal. This got *us* off the hook with the feds, but it didn't get the *network* off; they were the ones who now appeared guilty of an FCC violation.

So CBS agreed to investigate itself, and guess what: it found itself innocent of any malicious wrongdoing. Eventually, the FCC let the matter pass and the whole issue blew over.

However, a new era of 'awareness' was created, and the networks became much more cautious about what was said on the air and about the manner in which they promoted their events. And 'winner take all' became a dirty phrase in television sports.

One other side effect was that Barry Frank had become so fed up with the politics of the 'network game' that he resigned from CBS and rejoined IMG, where he eventually helped to collect $80,000 from the original suit against Bill Riordan!

And so a complicated chapter in the network television business ended with almost everyone happy and maybe even a bit wiser.

The Gypsy's Curse

One final reason to think long and hard before initiating what might be thought of as a 'discretionary lawsuit' is suggested by an old gypsy curse of truly devilish insight: 'May you be involved in a lawsuit in which you are in the right.'

The evil gist of this malediction, of course, is contained in the idea of being the innocent party.

If you're in the *wrong*, after all, what have you got to lose? The *worst* that can happen is that justice will be done.

Anything short of justice and the bad guy is ahead while the good guy comes up short.

But who's 'ahead' as long as the result is still pending?

It seems clear that **the side that has committed the injury maintains an unfair advantage through all the months or years it takes to get a lawsuit settled.**

The party that has been wronged is *still* being wronged, is still *aggrieved* about the wrong, and is still spending time and money to have the wrong undone.

Viewed in this light, stalling tactics are not just a way of suspending the action, but of *compounding* the injury.

And the person who brings suit, by opening himself to the sort of delays and complications we have discussed, *allows* the injury to be compounded.

True, he may recoup his losses and have his sweet revenge eventually.

But *eventually* can be an awfully long time coming. And I will testify from personal experience that there are times when long-awaited victories seem oddly hollow when they finally occur.

For all those reasons, I would urge that every potential suitor ask himself three questions:

Can I afford to lose?

Can I afford to wait perhaps a decade or more for a resolution?

Could I perhaps more easily afford – both financially and emotionally – to swallow my losses, dust off my dignity, and get on with my life?

10

Something's Gotta Give

Remember the famous *Pennzoil v. Texaco* case?

In that monumental litigation of 1986, Pennzoil claimed that Texaco had unfairly bought Getty Oil out from under them, and was awarded an epoch-making judgment of $10.5 billion!

Now, this book is not the place to mull over the merits of the case, or do more than wonder about the possible justification for such a gargantuan award.

But there is one point I would like to make about *Pennzoil v. Texaco*.

The stock market is supposedly an accurate and efficient mechanism for separating winners and losers, and for keeping score in the matter of national wealth. In a head-to-head battle between two companies, then, you would expect that one corporation's loss would equal the other's gain.

But in fact, after the *Pennzoil v. Texaco* decision, the total value of Texaco's stock shrank considerably more than the worth of Pennzoil's stock increased. The *net* loss was around $2.1 billion!

Where did that $2 billion go?

In *legal fees*, quipped one Wall Street pundit.

The remark, of course, is not literally true. Not even oil giants pay *that* much to their attorneys.

What is painfully true, however, as dramatically illustrated by *Pennzoil v. Texaco*, is that **litigation is nearly always a drain on wealth.**

It is an economic as well as an emotional depressant.

Further, this is true whether gigantic corporations are

battling it out for billions, or whether the estranged Mr and Mrs Jones are fighting to see who keeps the cottage. The terrible truth is that **the net result is virtually always a loss.**

No new riches are created by a lawsuit. Lawsuits don't drill oil wells or build bungalows. Lawsuits don't bring products to consumers or buoy up the economies of summer communities.

All that lawsuits accomplish – sometimes – is transferring money from party A to party B.

In the process of being forked over, however, a portion of that money sticks to the fingers of the lawyers – who are *outside* the circle of the original conflict.

Therefore, the net result almost invariably is that wealth is taken *out* of a given system – whether the system is industry or the domestic economy of the Joneses.

And, as anyone with the slightest bit of common sense will realize, you can't take wealth out of the system forever, without making the system go broke. Which is why something's gotta give with legal practice, Western-style.

Where Will It All End?

Item: More than twelve million lawsuits are filed each year in the United States. Given that there are at least two parties to a suit, that works out roughly to one action for every dozen men, women and children in the country.

Item: Everyone talks about the debilitating effects of the US trade imbalance and budget deficits. But no one seems to be aware that the federal government has a liability burden that runs to similar amounts. At this writing, there are roughly forty thousand civil actions pending against the government, and their total damage claims add up to an unbelievable $139 billion.

At least for our trade deficit, we get in exchange cars, steel and television sets!

Item: Lloyd's of London, perhaps the world's most famous risk takers – a company that has written life insurance for wing-walkers and climbers of Mount Everest – recently dropped out of the American liability reinsurance game.

198

Their reasoning? The US market is no longer just risky; it's simply a no-win proposition.

Lawsuits Nobody Wants

The above items make plain what most of us already know: we have too damn many lawsuits on our hands, and most of them don't do anyone, except the lawyers, much good.

How did this sorry state of affairs come about in the first place?

Part of the answer lies in the old quip about the peaceful little town that didn't have enough business to support a lawyer – but had more than enough to support *two*.

Lawyers don't just *service* legal business; they *create* it.

Like any other successful group with a product it would like to sell, *attorneys don't just feed a need, they breed a need.*

Their mere presence inclines people to think in terms of settling differences legalistically. And contemporary America has more laywers around than any society has ever produced in the history of the world.

Where the Buck Stops

The temptation, then, is to say that we have too many lawsuits because we have too many lawyers.

But that's too easy.

A lawyer doesn't sue unless he has a client.

More specifically, a lawyer doesn't sue unless he has a client who *wants* to sue.

The word 'wants', however, is a tricky one. What a client 'wants' is partly conditioned by the prestige and power of the lawyers.

A client may 'want' to sue because a lawyer persuades him that he *should* sue. An opportunistic attorney may dangle pound signs in front of a prospective plaintiff's eyes. A shrewd practitioner may imply that a client is a wimp if he 'takes this lying down'.

Lawyers, like the rest of us, are salesmen.

Ultimately, though, it is the client's choice to buy or not to

199

buy what the lawyer is selling. **Ultimately, it is the client's decision whether a given conflict goes as far as litigation.**

But that decision is a weighty one, and causes a lot of anxiety. And because of the anxiety, *the decision is too often made not on the basis of positive action, but of passivity.*

What do I mean by that?

Let's say, for example, that one of our line executives has negotiated a contract that is eventually broken by the other side. Our legal department contacts the executive to learn more about the history of the deal and to get his input on how to proceed. But now the executive is busy with other things. Or he can no longer remember all the details. Or he doesn't *want* to remember all the details. So he tells Legal to handle it as they see fit.

Like Pilate washing his hands, the executive *should know* the likely course of events. Left to themselves, the lawyers will probably sue; *that's what they assume their job to be.* And the executive has *passively* made the decision to go ahead with the suit.

– Every time a business person tells a lawyer, 'I'm too busy; you handle it,' he is asking for a lawsuit.

– Every time an aggrieved individual tells an attorney, 'I get too upset to deal with it; do what you think best,' he is opening himself to having his life taken over by the courts.

The bottom line is that, while we may all moan about lawsuits none of us wants, ultimately it's usually our own fault when, by inattention, poor judgement, or the inability to say no, we find ourselves embroiled in legal squabbles.

When Is Delegating More Than Delegating?

I'm only too aware of this dynamic because I have got caught up in it myself on more than one occasion, usually just by stretching myself too thin.

It is a congenital defect of deal makers that they would rather pay attention to the next deal than to the last one.

It is also true that life is very complicated and it's impossible to take care of everything at once.

So, for example, if I'm negotiating a deal in Sydney, and a licensing arrangement goes sour in Paris, the Paris problem isn't going to get very much of my personal attention. I will delegate somebody else to take care of it; or someone else will do it *automatically*, in keeping with the standard practices of our organization.

This, however, leads to the following axiom:

> ## McCormack's Axiom of Delegating Versus More-than-delegating
>
> Delegating authority to another executive is one thing; delegating authority to a lawyer is quite another.

Why?

Because something done by a lower-ranking executive can nearly always be *undone* if necessary. Usually there are mechanisms by which someone can be gone over or got around without a loss of face or employment. And in extreme cases, an executive *faux pas* can almost always be erased by firing the executive; there is an unwritten rule among business people that firing the wrongdoer eliminates the wrong, and we can all be friends again once X has got the chop.

With lawyers, matters are very different. You can't blithely call in a more senior lawyer to unsay the nasty things a more junior lawyer has said in a civil complaint. You can't make a lawsuit vanish just by firing the attorney who launched it.

In a very real way, **when you pass matters on to an attorney, you're not just delegating authority; you're surrendering it.**

To Spite Your Face

Let me give you an example of the kinds of things that happen when executives take a see-no-evil, hear-no-evil approach to problems and passively let the lawyers do things their own way.

201

A number of years ago, a disagreement sprang up between our client Bjorn Borg, at the time the undisputed number one tennis player in the world, and Lamar Hunt, one of the world's wealthiest men and the promoter of World Championship Tennis tournaments. To put a rather complex matter simply, Hunt and Borg disagreed about whether Borg would play WCT tournaments and on what basis.

IMG executives didn't monitor this situation as closely as they might have. Neither, apparently, did Lamar Hunt himself. Probably neither side imagined that the other would be stupid enough to let this skirmish escalate into a war.

So the matter was handed over to the attorneys to resolve, and the next thing we knew Hunt and Borg were suing each other!

If ever there was a case of two parties cutting off their respective noses, this was it. The world's best tennis player and the world's biggest tennis promoter were at an impasse at the precise moment in history when tennis's growth curve was at its steepest!

Hunt and Borg were natural allies in a hugely profitable enterprise – what did either have to gain by fighting? With or without Borg, Hunt would be vastly wealthy and tremendously powerful; with or without Hunt, Borg would still be the star of the tennis circuit. No way did Borg have the leverage to lord it over Hunt, nor could Hunt coerce Borg into *performing*, as opposed to just showing up, at his tournaments.

Hunt and Borg together, on almost *any* basis, made a more potent and profitable entity than Hunt and Borg at odds.

The lawyers, however, didn't see it that way. Hunt's attorneys, who were all on staff in any case, seemed inclined to pursue the action to the bitter end. Borg's lawyers – who had been hired *ad hoc* and were costing Bjorn a fortune – were equally belligerent.

Neither side apparently conceived that the purpose was to *resolve* the matter. Each saw itself as *winning* – irrespective of the fact that there was essentially nothing to be won!

There had to be a better way of dealing with the matter,

and I decided to hop on a plane to Texas and talk to Lamar Hunt directly.

Hunt greeted me with an 'aw shucks' manner that seemed at odds with his wealth and influence until you realized that the informality was coupled with an incredibly keen attentiveness; he kept things homey, the better to observe what was *really* going on.

After a few minutes of talking around the problem, Hunt told me, in effect, that he didn't have much stomach for this battle, but he just plain didn't like a man who welshed on his obligations.

Now, Bjorn Borg never welshed on an obligation in his life; that wasn't what was going on now, and I told Hunt that.

In the same moment, Hunt and I both realized what *had* been going on. *His* lawyers had been portraying Borg as trying to weasel out of the commitment he had made to the WCT; *Borg*'s lawyer had been portraying Hunt as bullheaded and inaccessible to compromise. Neither side was right.

It's not that the lawyers were *lying*, but they were looking at the problem through what might be called *the lens of litigiousness*, and that is what they saw.

Hunt and I looked at the problem differently: through a *business* lens.

Within an hour we were able to work out the framework of an agreement that put an end to the lawsuit and got the Hunt-Borg relationship back on track.

The thing I want to stress, however, is that the settlement I was able to strike with Lamar Hunt *did not* have to do with any negotiating razzle-dazzle. There were no trump cards, no new factors, nothing mysterious.

The success of our meeting, in fact, probably had less to do with substantive issues than with *the spirit in which it was entered into.*

We were intent on being cooperative, not adversarial. We were determined to be gracious, not belligerent. As business-men, we settled the matter in terms of costs and benefits, not egos, actions and billable hours.

This is not to say that business people are intrinsically more

203

reasonable than lawyers. Clearly, there are two sides to *that* argument!

The difference, rather, is one of the context:

The lawyer's natural context is one of conflict.
The business person's natural context is one of mutual advantage.

Letting matters drift from the latter view to the former is asking for ill will.

A Brief Crusade

Throughout this book, I have tried my damnedest to stay off the soapbox. I have been at constant pains to keep the focus on real, immediate problems with real, practical solutions, and to steer clear of flights of theory, utopian visions, and just plain howling in frustration that the legal system doesn't work better than it does.

But I would be shirking a responsibility if I didn't say at least a little bit about possible reforms in legal practice.

The word 'reform', I realize, is a loaded one – it carries all sorts of ideological baggage and it tends to make conservatives rush to the barricades.

But the kinds of reform I'm talking about have nothing to do with ideology, and everything to do with practical results:

– I would like to see lawyers *expedite* the conduct of business rather than slow it down.

– I would like to see lawyers settle disputes in such a way that profits are enhanced, rather than drained.

– I would like to see the courts regain their dignity as places where *actual* wrongs are *fairly* redressed, not where seven-figure handouts are thrown around in an atmosphere like that of a TV game show.

As I hope this book has managed to convey, **the system in its current state serves the lawyers better than it serves the rest of us.**

For that reason, the bar has a clear vested interest in maintaining the status quo, and they guard that interest with

204

a passion. Anyone who has ever imagined trying to take a nice meaty bone away from a pack of Dobermans will have an idea of the difficulty of getting lawyers to accede to meaningful reform.

Still, change begins with awareness, and awareness comes about by people speaking up. So here goes.

The Worst of All Possible Worlds

As things currently stand, lawyers get paid according to two ways of reckoning, and both of them are bad.

— Either way they get paid for time, which encourages inefficiency, stalling, needless confrontations, over-lawyering and contentiousness.

— Or they get paid on contingency, which encourages frivolous suits, dubious tactics, appeals to emotion rather than to reason, and sheer runaway greed.

Not only are these compensation methods suspect in themselves, but the way in which they are applied sometimes strikes me as backward.

Typically, of course, plaintiffs' lawyers work on contingency, and defendants' lawyers work on time.

The theory behind this — worthy enough — is that no one should be prevented from prosecuting a meritorious claim because of a lack of funds. In practice, however, truly needy plaintiffs tend to be excluded *anyway*, for a couple of reasons.

First of all, there are almost always *some* up-front costs to be borne; second, suing entails at least a certain degree of power, and it's the indigent who are most likely to be lacking the requisite knowledge and resources.

So the plaintiff-contingency system doesn't truly help those who *can't* afford legal help; it just gives a free ride to those who *can*.

Now look at it from the other side:

By forcing defendants to pay their lawyers on a time basis, the system *presumes* that defendants have deep pockets. Further, although the plaintiff bears the burden of demonstrating that a wrong has been done – the civil-law equivalent of being 'innocent till proven guilty' – the defendant is effectively being penalized from the first tick of the legal meter.

Our Own Grey Panther

Let me give you a brief example of this lopsided logic in action.

A few years ago, IMG was sued by a former employee who claimed that she had been fired because of age discrimination – she was fifty-five. In fact, she was fired because, within a few months of being hired, it became clear that she had lied about her skills and experience.

Nevertheless, the woman was aggrieved, and she went out and got herself a lawyer. The lawyer no doubt felt he had a highly marketable client on his hands – a sweet, well-spoken, silver-haired woman who was bound to make a hit with a jury.

The lawyer informed us that we were being sued for $3 million! Why not? Under our legal system, **it costs no more to file a moonshot claim than a reasonable one.**

A small proportion of the amount was based on income the woman *would have earned*, had she worked until she was sixty-five. The rest was punitive damages, on the grounds that we had put a black mark on her record, or hurt her feelings, or something equally vague.

Now, at IMG, as at most companies, we have a procedure to follow when we get sued. The procedure is complicated, time-consuming, and it takes our in-house lawyers away from work that *makes* money, but we can't afford not to follow it.

We review the claim. We research our own files and talk to people within the company to ascertain, first of all, if we are actually at fault, and second, how strong a case could be made against us. Then we decide how to proceed. If the case seems likely to go to trial, we hire outside counsel to litigate.

In the present instance, we were sure we were blameless, and confident that we could not convincingly be portrayed as otherwise. Accordingly, our legal department wrote a letter

206

to the other side, suggesting that this matter did not warrant litigation, and urging that our ex-employee's lawyer submit the case to labour arbitration instead.

But the lawyer was adamant. He knew that with this likable woman, whose feelings were hurt and whose self-esteem had been shaken, his best chance – his *only* chance – lay in pulling the heartstrings of a jury.

So the suit went ahead and, to cut a long story short, we eventually 'won'. Our so-called victory cost us $50,000 in fees and expenses. For better or worse, however, we weren't the only party to come out behind. The woman lost, too, since she had put in all that time and trouble for nothing. Even her lawyer lost, since he had no moonshot payday at the end. The only *real* winners were *our* outside lawyers, who made their hourly rate no matter what.

It seems to me there's something wrong with a system that takes three losers to add up to one winner.

Putting the Common Sense Back into Common Law

How might the situation be improved?

At least a few ideas can be had from going back to the source of much of our legal logic, English common law – which in turn derived from everyday, sensible practices that were already established by the time the law was codified.

Common law, then, is not a product of lawyers' self-serving ingenuity, but of *people trying their best to get along*.

Under common law, for example, *punitive damages were assessed only in cases where an injury was intentional; in other sorts of liability actions, the 'negligent' party would pay the doctor's bills, and that was pretty much all there was to it.*

In other words, *wrongs were redressed in a spirit of justice, not of revenge, opportunism, and misguided attempts to redistribute wealth.*

For better or worse, our culture has come to take very seriously such hazy concepts as 'mental distress' and 'pain and suffering'. The belief in those concepts, coupled with the feeling that an injured party is *entitled* to a payoff, makes it unrealistic to return to medical-expenses-only judgments.

But clearly, **a cap can and should be placed on awards for non-physical or non-economic damages.**

Laws to this effect have already been passed in several American states, with $250,000 – not a small amount – being a typical ceiling for 'pain and suffering' awards. I would urge that these ceilings be universally adopted.

Needless to say, lawyers are fighting them to the bitter end.

Fighting Fair

Another element of common law that should be resurrected in America is that **losers in civil actions should pay the legal costs of the winners,** as happens in the UK.

This, if you think about it, would only be fair, whether the suit is ultimately decided in favour of the plaintiff or the defendant.

Looking at it from the defendant's perspective, no one *asks* to be sued, and the mere fact of having to participate in a lawsuit is already a species of punishment. If the lawsuit turns out to be frivolous or groundless, should one have to pay legal fees as well?

Common sense cries out a resounding no. Under the English system, defendants at least have the comfort of knowing they won't go broke in the process of demonstrating their innocence.

Conversely, plaintiffs are discouraged from lodging unmeritorious claims because there's no such thing as a free ride if they lose.

Both sides are at risk in an English civil action – which is another way of saying it's a fair fight.

If the plaintiff *does* win, the English system still makes perfect sense. The defendant is ordered to pay the plaintiff's legal fees *separately* from the judgment.

Thus there is no ambiguity about what the size of the award really is, and no confusion about who is benefiting from it and to what degree. The process is clean, explicit and fair.

The Fly in the Ointment

These provisions are so clearly equitable and workable that the only mystery is why they *haven't* been enacted in the United States.

The answer, I strongly suspect, has to do with *another* practice in the English courts, corollary to the above.

Under the English system, legal fees are determined by expert officers of the courts (taxing masters) and are based on complexity, involvement and the importance, monetarily or otherwise, of the matter to the client. The fees assessed by English courts, it should be understood, are reasonable but subject at all times to scrutiny by officers of the courts. Still, English practitioners are not generally awarded quite the princely sums that American attorneys routinely chalk up for themselves, on their own recognizance and at their own discretion.

The terrible truth, apparently, is that the American legal profession has no inclination to adopt a system that would better serve the public, in place of one that so admirably serves itself.

Some Glimmers of Hope

Still, even though fully-fledged legal reform is probably too much to hope for in the near future, there seem to be certain positive stirrings among the many executives and lawyers I have occasion to deal with.

These stirrings have to do not with changes in statutes, but in changes in *attitudes*.

There is an East Coast clothier whose motto is An Educated Consumer Is Our Best Customer.

Well, *legal* customers, too, are becoming better educated these days, and as they do, they are becoming more adept at steering clear of the worst horrors of the system.

They become better versed, as it were, in *guerrilla tactics* that enable them to achieve legal objectives without the grinding, plodding 'conventional warfare' of litigation.

What are these guerrilla tactics?

Preventive Lawyering

'Preventive lawyering' is really what Abraham Lincoln was talking about in one of the quotations that serve as the epigraph of this book.

Honest Abe exhorted his fellow attorneys to 'discourage litigation' and implement conciliation, pointing out that a lawyer's 'superior opportunity' lay not in waging surrogate battles, but in serving as a 'peacemaker'.

Well, that's wonderful advice, but there's a basic problem with it: it flies in the face of how many Western lawyers have traditionally made their money.

Under the American and most European systems, those attorneys grow wealthy by taking conflicts to the hilt rather than by avoiding conflicts. It's worth remembering, however, that there *are* other ways to set things up.

Consider this analogy with medicine. Western societies pay doctors essentially on the same basis that they pay lawyers: for dealing with the 'disease' once something has gone wrong.

In Eastern societies, however, doctors are paid *not* for curing someone when he's sick, *but for keeping him healthy in the first place*. In traditional China, for example, if you got sick, your doctor treated you for free, on the supposition that if he had been doing his job well, you wouldn't have become ill. You paid him if you stayed healthy – *there was a direct correlation between the charge and the benefit.*

We Westerners do things backwards! We pay nothing for the benefits of 'health' – medical or legal – and we pay like crazy for the 'privilege' of being sick or being sued!

Since that's the quality of 'logic' we are stuck with, I suppose it follows 'logically' that Western attorneys conduct themselves less like statesmen and peacemakers than like bodyguards and *agents provocateurs*.

Increasingly, however, companies and individuals are finding that **legal help can be a worthwhile investment before something goes wrong.**

– Corporations are looking to lawyers to *steer them clear* of things like environmental violations or product-liability suits, rather than to *defend* them afterwards.

— Small businessmen are becoming savvier in using lawyers *early* to avoid later problems with taxes or partnerships that go sour.

— Increasing numbers of couples are hiring lawyers to write prenuptial agreements to avoid ugly and expensive battles in case of divorce.

The growth of preventive lawyering, of course, will have everything to do with the *demand* for preventive lawyering. And that demand, in turn, can come only from an increasingly sophisticated clientele.

Once you know how much it costs to end up in court, you realize what a bargain it can be to pay someone to keep you out of court.

Alternative Dispute Resolution

Not long ago I had occasion to hear the words of a man named Peter Kaskell, formerly the general counsel of the Olin Corporation, and now senior vice president of a public-service organization called the Center for Public Resources.

CPR is probably the nation's most prestigious promoter of alternatives to litigation, boasting on its judicial panel such august figures as Watergate prosecutor Archibald Cox, former Attorney General Griffin Bell, and former Health, Education and Welfare Secretary Joseph Califano.

Kaskell quoted some facts and figures that I found astonishing:

— As of late 1986, *more than half* the companies that comprise the Fortune 500 had signed a pledge saying that they would try to use less expensive, less time-consuming alternatives to litigation in conflicts with each other.

— More than twenty-five major insurance companies had signed a similar commitment.

— In all, companies accounting for more than one quarter of the entire US GNP had promised to take all reasonable steps to stay out of court against each other.

211

Given that conflicts among these companies are inevitable, how will they manage to avoid full-blown litigation? By turning instead to such forms of settlement as mediation, arbitration, 'mini-trials', 'private' trials, and other pragmatic techniques that have not traditionally been taught in law schools, and that come under the umbrella of 'alternative dispute resolution', or ADR.

Why are the general counsels of Fortune 500 companies so high on these techniques for staying out of court? Because they know a few things that most of us *don't*:

– Many an expensive and bitter lawsuit comes about *not* because of substantive issues, but simply because two people with some power have got angry with each other!

– Too many executives *think* they have had a 'negotiation', when in fact all they have done is to yell at each other over the telephone, getting worked up enough to throw the file disgustedly into the legal department's lap.

– Once the *principals* in a conflict stop talking, the chances of settling become radically slimmer.

– Arbitration or a 'mini-trial' will cost their companies about one tenth as much as litigation.

– All of which says, they understand the *psychology* of conflicts, and how to use that psychology to *save* money and time rather than squander them.

It's beyond the scope of this book to talk about all the different forms of ADR, but let me relate one anecdote that summarizes the dynamics that are typically involved.

Back before the 1984 Winter Olympics at Sarajevo, Yugoslavia, IMG was doing everything possible to cement our relationships with contacts in Yugoslavia. Obviously, we wanted to enhance our connections so as to secure as big a slice as possible of the promotional and TV-production pie.

Around this time, we were approached by an individual with whom we had done *some* business before. He was a very well-travelled adventurer, sometime journalist, and entrepreneur. He had lived for a time in Eastern Europe, and made a very impressive pitch about the sort of entrée he could provide for us in Yugoslavia.

His pitch was *so* impressive that we arranged to have him accompany one of our executives to Europe, and we agreed to give him a 10 per cent cut of any commissions we received from the Sarajevo event.

Well, it turned out that this fellow's star contact hadn't even *been* in Yugoslavia for fifteen years! His other connections and expertise turned out to be only slightly less worthless.

In the meantime, through our executives' own diligence and ingenuity, we ended up doing very well in Sarajevo and the Winter Olympics were quite profitable for us.

So we decided to give our 'envoy' $25,000 for his (limited) time and (limited) trouble – and frankly I thought we were being damn generous under the circumstances.

Far from being too embarrassed to cash the cheque, however, the fellow informed us that he wanted the entire 10 per cent, and that if we didn't pay up, he would sue us!

An odd and perverse thing happens when litigation looms that I call:

McCormack's Axiom of Sudden Virtue

In the face of a court battle, both sides become almost instantly convinced that they are not just right, but *righteous*, and flexibility vanishes.

To prevent this happening, we suggested submitting the conflict to a 'mini-trial'. A mini-trial is a procedure whereby the parties to a disagreement, usually but not necessarily accompanied by their lawyers, sit down to present their case to a neutral 'judge' – usually a lawyer, though it could be anyone skilled in the art of mediation. The 'judge' hears the presentations, then renders a 'verdict' – i.e., gives his advised opinion of how the case *would* turn out if it did go to court.

The results of mini-trials are nonbinding. However, in the overwhelming majority of instances, they lead to speedy

213

settlements *because they undo the Axiom of Stubbornness*. Opinions coming from a *neutral source* are acceptable, when *those same opinions*, coming from an adversary, would be scorned.

In the present instance, the 'judge' said essentially, 'McCormack, you cut yourself a dumb deal this time because the agreement was pegged to *results*, and not to *means*, and therefore you'd probably lose. However, a jury would probably realize that this fellow hasn't earned anything like the full commission, and I suggest you settle on a figure somewhere in between.'

In the end, we gave him $40,000.

No one likes to give away that much money, but look at it this way: if we had gone to court, forty thousand *might* have covered our legal fees. On top of that, a jury might have awarded the full amount – who knows? Finally, this fellow and I would have been mad at each other for that much longer.

Business people, by and large, don't like to hold grudges; it's not in their interest. And one of the worst things about lawsuits is that they make conflict a habit.

How to Think Like a Lawyer
(Without Hating Yourself
in the Morning)

Every honest book, whatever its apparent subject, is really a book about human nature.

This volume is no exception. And my intuitions about human nature lead me to suspect that, even though most of what I have said about lawyers has been less than complimentary, what many people will want to carry away from these pages is a sense of how they can be more *like* lawyers.

Lawyers, for all the criticisms that I and countless other observers have levelled against them, still feel pretty darn good about being members of the bar. They tend also to be oddly proud about being generally disliked and avoided like the plague.

And a fair proportion of nonlawyers continue to be more than a little intrigued and envious, not to say impressed or even awed, by attorneys.

Why?

In a word, because lawyers – skilled ones – are *effective*.

In their own way, they get things done – and in fact what looks from the outside like stalling or inaction is often the most efficacious playing out of *the lawyer's own agenda*.

Skilled lawyers can be brilliant at defining the rules of the game and making other people play within their boundaries. So, in accordance with another axiom:

> ### McCormack's Axiom of Ground Rules
> If you can be the one to establish the terms of play, you have already gone a long way towards winning.

Winning is what people admire, albeit grudgingly, about attorneys.

When possible, attorneys win on behalf of their clients; come what may; however, they almost always win on behalf of *themselves*.

And this capacity to turn almost any situation to advantage is what so many nonlawyers would like to be able to emulate. So how can they?

The Four Cornerstones

To begin answering that question, let's come back to the four basic lawyering skills – Interviewing, Counselling, Negotiating and Drafting.

As we said earlier, these four abilities form the bedrock on which lawyers really operate, and yet **they aren't generally taught in law school!**

Which means, among other things, that attorneys haven't got a lock or even necessarily a meaningful headstart on the learning and application of these abilities.

These skills are partly intuitive and partly gathered from real-life experience – whether it comes from legal practice or business practice or, for that matter, almost any arena where a premium is placed on:

– listening carefully;
– reading people accurately;
– thinking logically;
– writing clearly; and
– being open to creative and sometimes oblique solutions.

Interviewing

A journalist friend once told me that the most exhausting aspect of his job was not writing, but interviewing the subjects of his stories. A two-hour interview, he said, left him wrung out – and made him realize that, by contrast, people barely pay attention to each other in the course of normal conversation.

– In everyday chitchat, nuances go unnoticed, points are ignored, threads get lost.

– Opportunities to zero in on ideas are wasted for want of concentration.

– Chances for clarification go by the board because people's 'conversational reflexes' aren't quick enough to seize them.

What interviewing *is* – whether done by a reporter on the trail of a story, a lawyer in the service of a client, or a business person in pursuit of a deal – is a highly specialized, highly energized and highly active mode of listening.

Interviewing, done right, *is* exhausting because it calls into play a number of faculties at once.

Hearing what someone says is only part of it.

There is also a sort of 'listening' that one does with the eyes.

What statements, for example, does your opposite number feel strongly enough about to reinforce with emphatic gestures? At what junctures does he try for eye contact, and when does he look away? Does he lean forward aggressively while making his points, or does he settle back against his chair?

If he is taking notes, what are the sort of things he seems to be writing down? Does he appear to be most interested in numbers or ideas? On what topics does his attention seem most crisply focused, and when does it become diffuse?

What makes him squirm?

All these various observations need to be filtered through the mill of intuition, and synthesized into *a responsive awareness of what the other party really wants from you* – whether the interview is between a lawyer and a client, or between a vendor and a potential customer in a business situation.

That may sound obvious, but in fact it isn't obvious at all **because what the other party seems to want from you, and what he or she really wants, are often two different things.**

Let me illustrate this point by way of an example. A few years ago, I was approached by a very well-known sports broadcaster who was interested in getting IMG to represent him, and I suggested we met for a talk.

This announcer had previously been represented by another agent with whom he had become disenchanted. Having had representation before, he was quite sophisticated, knew all the jargon, and was savvy and articulate enough to ask all the right questions.

If I went *only* by his words, I would have concluded that he was a highly businesslike person who wanted an agent to make him the best deals and make him the most money, period.

His posture and gestures, however, told a somewhat different story.

During almost the whole conversation, this individual leaned forward across my desk, made gestures across the space between us, and at moments seemed almost as if he wanted to tug at my cuff while making a point.

It didn't take a Doctor Freud to realize that, while the ostensible subject of our chat was contracts and money, its *subtext* was this announcer's need to feel personal concern and warmth coming from his agent, to feel that he would get emotional as well as business support from the person who represented him.

This, I stress, would not have been remotely evident from a transcript of our talk; it had everything to do with the *visual* side of listening.

By paying attention to what this fellow was *showing* me as well as what he was telling me, I was able to address what he *really* wanted from me.

Sure, he wanted the best business advice he could find; the emotional side in no way negated that, but just added another element. By responding to his unstated as well as his stated needs, I was able to forge a relationship that still continues.

218

Counselling

We all know the old quip about free advice being worth exactly what you pay for it.

For all that, most of us still love to give advice – first of all, because it's flattering to be consulted, and second, because it's generally less unpleasant to think about someone else's dilemma than about one's own.

Similarly, most of us probably find ourselves *asking* for advice (whether or not we have the faintest intention of following it!), if for no other reason than that life is sometimes so mystifying that it can't hurt to have a second opinion.

Lawyers make their living, in large part, from the giving of advice, or counselling. They are thus in the enviable position of being very handsomely paid for an activity that most of us jump at the chance to do gratis.

Therefore, one should keep in mind this rule:

McCormack's Axiom of Expert Opinion

The notion that free advice is worth nothing does not suggest that expensive advice is necessarily worth a lot. It depends on who's giving the advice, not on the amount of money being shelled out for the privilege of receiving it.

Whether or not someone is paid to give advice *next* time has a lot to do with what that person's advice turned out to be worth *last* time.

Attorneys are paid for counselling because of the things they *do* learn in law school. They are privy to a body of knowledge on which they are uniquely qualified to have opinions.

But the *psychology* of counselling is the common property of everyone – agents, salespeople, brokers, managers – for whom giving sound advice is part of doing business.

What, then, are the essential components of effective counselling?

First of all, **effective interviewing.** As we will see, each of the four basic skills delineated here feeds on all the others, and you obviously can't give someone sound advice unless you have listened carefully to what his problem is.

The next step in effective counselling is **separating the other party's best interests from your own.**

In some situations, of course, both parties' interests are perfectly aligned; that is a best-case scenario that makes advice-giving and decision-making blessedly simple.

Usually, however, situations aren't quite so cut-and-dried.

Let's say I am approached by a manufacturer, with whom I have not done business before, who would like to retain one of IMG's clients as an endorser of his product.

Clearly, this is of benefit both to the client and to the company. We will both make money in the short run. And in the long run, the company will presumably benefit from starting a new relationship that might bring in other business in the future.

But what if this deal isn't *absolutely the best* we could get for the client? What if we could get even *marginally* better terms from a competing manufacturer with whom we already worked – in which case IMG would sacrifice the additional benefit of opening up new territory?

What would I counsel my client to do?

It so happens that agents have an explicit ethical and legal responsibility to play a fiduciary role, so the decision would be clear: I would counsel the choice that was best for the client, and mourn *my* lost opportunity in private.

However, what if I were operating in a domain where there was no such well-defined fiduciary role?

What if I were an air-conditioning salesman who would make X pounds in commission if I sold a customer the unit he really needed, or $2X$ pounds if I could get him to take the next model up? What would I counsel the customer then?

There are two issues here, one moral and one pragmatic.

The moral issue comes down to whether you want to do business on the basis of let the buyer beware, or whether you believe in the ethic of service. Personally, I have always felt that **good service and good salesmanship go together.**

Purely practically, the decision comes down to whether one is more interested in the quick score or in repeat business.

It is a quirk of human nature, I believe, that many of us spout off advice rather lightly, *but we* receive *advice with the utmost seriousness. We remember where the advice came from, and if it turns out to be bad, we remember whom to blame!*

Advice, in other words, carries with it *accountability*, and advice that in the long run is shown to have been self-serving is one of the surest ways to breed ill will.

On the other hand, one of the surest ways to breed *good*will and to cement loyalty is to do the sort of counselling that makes it clear that one is putting the other party's best interests ahead of one's own. There is no better or fairer way of making someone feel indebted.

I heard a story once which illustrates this point. A friend of mine was about to invest a substantial sum of money through a broker with whom he had done only a small amount of business before.

Between the time the investment was decided upon, however, and the time it was actually executed, the expected yield on the investment dropped by *one quarter of a per cent.*

The broker dutifully ran the new numbers, then called my friend to tell him that the investment was no longer his best bet, and counselled him instead to make a move that entailed *a far smaller sales charge.*

My friend was momentarily flabbergasted. But if you don't think he'll bring that broker a lot more business in the future, then you haven't been paying attention either to this book or to real-life human beings!

Negotiating

In a broad sense, every page of this book has been about the art of negotiating.

Whether the issue has been getting Gary Player the most advantageous endorsement deal on golf clubs, or putting Bjorn Borg and WCT back on track, or freeing the Royal

Perth Yacht Club from interference in exploiting its ownership of the America's Cup – all these situations have entailed the mediation between competing interests, with an eye towards a mutually profitable, face-saving, and, whenever possible, relationship-preserving result.

Human beings, whether they are aware of it or not, are negotiating all the time.

When you ask a waitress if you can substitute a second vegetable for a baked potato, that's a negotiation. When you suggest to the garage attendant that he can have the business of waxing your car if he gives you fast in-out service, that's a negotiation.

Leave it to lawyers, however, to take this natural, universal activity, and to formalize it with a lot of technical jargon and written or unwritten rules. While much of the jargon is utter nonsense, some of it happens to be useful.

Consider, for instance, the three categories into which attorneys divide negotiations: cooperative, adversarial and hostile.

The first category is self-explanatory: a cooperative negotiation is one in which the two parties' interests are more or less aligned and it is a given fact that both sides want to come to terms. The haggling is over *emphasis and details*, rather than over basic issues.

It is the distinction between the other two categories, however, that is interesting, *and far too often overlooked – in business, in the press, and even in diplomacy.*

An adversarial negotiation and a hostile negotiation are two different things, and only bad feelings and splitting headaches can come from confusing the two.

Probably the classic instance of an adversarial negotiation that is misconstrued – *and therefore mishandled* – as hostile is the bargaining that goes on between labour and management at contract time.

Clearly, this is a case in which the two sides have widely differing agendas. Moreover, since the executives and the unions are essentially haggling over slices of the very same

222

pie, they are involved in a zero-sum game, where one side's gain almost certainly comes at the expense of the other. This scenario makes for spirited debate, to put it mildly.

Still, it is a terrible mistake to think of the two sides as enemies. Each side – though it might cringe to admit this – *needs* the other.

Neither can afford to *alienate* the other.

The bottom line is that they will be doing business again. **And while their short-term interests are in conflict, their long-term interests are inextricably linked.**

If one side is made to lose face, both sides will eventually suffer.

If the negotiations conlude in a spirit of waiting for revenge, and not in a conciliation, nothing will have been accomplished.

A classic case of this labour-management snafu can be seen in the handling of the 1982 major-league baseball strike. Without rehashing all the details of that unfortunate episode, suffice it to say that it was conducted and concluded in an atmosphere of unproductive mistrust and lingering ill will. The 'settlement' wasn't truly a settlement at all, but just a temporary expedient for getting the players back on the field. The issues weren't really resolved and the wounds, far from being healed, were left to fester.

So it isn't surprising that the owners have been trying to take back most of what they conceded at that time, nor is it surprising that *another* strike has remained a constant possibility and could happen at any time. With due respect to the parties involved, the terrible truth is that that was a terrible negotiation.

Terrible – but not atypical.

In my business career, I have seen far too many negotiators *imagine* that they are being toughminded, when in fact they are merely being pigheaded.

They seem to think they're being 'strong' if they refuse to give ground, and 'weak' if they make accommodation. This, as I would hope is clear to any civilized person, is nonsense.

Insofar as the don't-give-an-inch mentality is *ever* appropriate, it is appropriate only in situations where negotiations are out-and-out hostile.

And those situations, in turn, are very few. To my mind, they occur *only* when one party's rights have clearly been violated before negotiations have begun.

If someone seizes hostages, then wants to talk, that's a hostile negotiation.

If one party to a contract reneges unconscionably, *then* wants to discuss the matter, that's a hostile negotiation.

Short of that, negotiations may be adversarial but still friendly, and should be approached on that basis.

You *don't* want to leave the other side bleeding on the floor.

You *do* want to leave the other side feeling that they've cut a good deal – while you have the quiet satisfaction of feeling that you've cut a better one!

I like to think that the anecdotes throughout this book have presented a versatile repertoire of tactics for achieving that result, so I won't labour the point further. However, by way of summing up, I would like to drive home just a few basic principles:

– TALK ISSUES, NOT EGOS

Everyone likes to feel important, and one of the great negotiating pitfalls is to go in thinking that one's own brilliance, clout and resourcefulness are the true subject of the proceedings.

Well, they're not.

The subject is a contract, or a renewal, or whatever: it is something *external*.

In a negotiation *everyone* is an agent, someone standing as spokesperson for a certain point of view. That's what I mean when I say that arguments are *schematic*.

Keep that in mind, and you won't trip over your own self-importance.

– DON'T GRANDSTAND

A trial lawyer banging his fist on the table and raising his voice to a shriek may be good theatre, but it's bad negotiation.

Don't play to an audience — either a third party or other members of your own team.

Just talk to your opposite number. Make yourself understood, not by extravagant gestures but by logical argument.

The more theatrical you become, the more the other side feels obliged to respond in kind. The danger, then, is that instead of a negotiation, you end up with a spectacle that features all the chest thumping and ham acting of pro wrestling — and accomplishes about as much.

– BE OPEN TO OBLIQUE SOLUTIONS

I say a hundred; you say fifty; we settle at seventy-five.

This is the simplest sort of compromise. It is also stupendously dull and breathtakingly unoriginal.

Still, it is the basic dynamic by which most negotiations are settled – *not because it's the best way, but because people look no further*.

Maybe there's a way to do a deal so that I come away with the effective value of a hundred, *and* you get off with the effective cost of fifty.

Maybe, for that matter, we're better off talking *less* about the numbers, and *more* about the intangible benefits *both* of us can get from the arrangement.

Rather than getting fixated on the concept of 'middle ground', maybe there's a way in which both of us can have *most* of what we want.

In savvy negotiations, two plus two sometimes *can* add up to five.

This is called synergy. It's also called the effective way of doing business.

Drafting

One of my first assignments as an associate with Arter, Hadden, was to assist in drawing up a rate-increase application on behalf of the Ohio Bell Telephone Company.

My colleagues and I spent hours and hours struggling to

word the document *concisely, consistently and simply*. We tried to turn four pages into one, four paragraphs into one, four phrases into one.

Ironically, my legal education both helped and hindered me in this process.

It had given me the basic tools to use the language effectively.

But on the other hand, it had made me so relentlessly sensitive to loopholes, formalities, and what-ifs that to say *anything* simply became a real challenge. At every comma I was in danger of falling into the deadly trap of legalese.

The exercise made me aware of the double challenge in composing any sort of document: **keep it simple, but make it complete.**

The tension between those two goals is not always easy to resolve. And sometimes it makes for the plodding, cliché-ridden tripe that is representative not only of bad legal writing, but of bad business writing, too.

Bad business writing, it must be said, is endemic. This is a shame, because **written communication can and should do more than merely convey information; it should help to forge a relationship.**

In college I had an English professor who drummed into us the notion that all writing is rhetoric — that is, writing is *always meant to persuade.*

I don't mean persuasion in the narrow sense of talking someone into something. Rather, I mean persuasion as *winning someone over to a certain way of looking at things, charming someone with incisiveness of thought and fluency of expression.*

To put the matter kindly, the terrible truth is that business writing usually falls far short of that.

Why?

For one thing, business people, chronically pressed for time, dash things off without sufficient regard for *what's at stake* whenever they put something on paper.

In this, executives would be wise to take a lesson from attorneys.

226

True, we all complain about how long it takes for lawyers to draft even a simple document; however, we don't always appreciate the care that goes into the drafting.

Lawyers are taught early on that a document does more than record facts; **it also reflects the quality of the mind of the person who wrote it.**

This goes for *any* sort of writing, and I believe it is the real reason why so many people find writing so terrifying.

A spoken comment can always be modified, conveniently misremembered, or disclaimed altogether. A written document is *there*. It can be referred to, examined, criticized.

It isn't just on the record, it *is* the record.

For that reason, I would urge all business people to take a cue from lawyers, and spend a little extra time to make damn sure that *every* piece of correspondence says what you want it to say, in a manner that represents you accurately.

Remember: if you don't think it sounds like you, it's going to sound insincere to the person who receives it.

And few things are more embarrassing than having to explain what you meant to say, to someone who has what you did say in his files!

'Grace Under Pressure'

Ernest Hemmingway liked lawyers less than he liked bull-fighters, fishing-boat captains or bartenders.

So maybe he would wince at having his famous definition of 'guts' applied to attorneys.

Still, there is no denying that *grace under pressure* is part of every successful lawyer's make-up, and emulating that grace is perhaps something that nonlawyers would most like to be able to do.

So how do attorneys do it?

How do litigators remain composed and logical in the face of needling from the other side and occasional browbeating from the bench?

How do professional negotiators remain focused on the

minutiae of contracts long after most of us would have lost our tempers or made disadvantageous trades?

How do lawyers, in the face of raised voices, raised blood pressure, and pounding temples, see an argument through to its conclusion?

Partly, it's their training – those hard-earned law school lessons that **for every argument there is a counterargument, and that, come what may, one should never be at a loss for words.**

But I would suggest that, aside from and prior to that training, there is an intuitive skill – *attainable in varying degrees by all of us* – that allows people to be graceful under the pressure of professional conflict.

This is the final point I would like to make and I believe it is so crucial that if the reader of this book carries away nothing except this single observation, it will still have been worthwhile: what allows skilled lawyers – and can allow all of us – to function well under great duress is *the ability to strike a balance between commitment and detachment.*

The effective professional – lawyer, executive, salesman – should be *wholly concentrated on and committed to* the fulfilment of his professional role.

All the while, however, he should be aware that he has a self *beyond* that role.

Attack me in negotiation, and you are not really attacking *me*; you are attacking the point of view that I, with all my attention and even passion, am representing.

Still, I am removed enough to be able to answer you calmly.

The balance between commitment and detachment is what allows for the quality we call poise.

And poise is something we instinctively admire: in athletes, in executives, in professionals.

A lawyer who has achieved true poise will never want for clients.

And business people who attain true poise will deal effectively with lawyers when they need to; better still, they will be able to minimize those occasions when they *have* to.

But poise, it should be said, is not really an end in itself. It's a stepping stone to a higher good: dignity.

Dignity is what poise *grows into* when it becomes second nature. And dignity – an *effective* dignity that lets us get things done not just with flair but with peace of mind – is really the ultimate object of the exercise.

INDEX

231

232